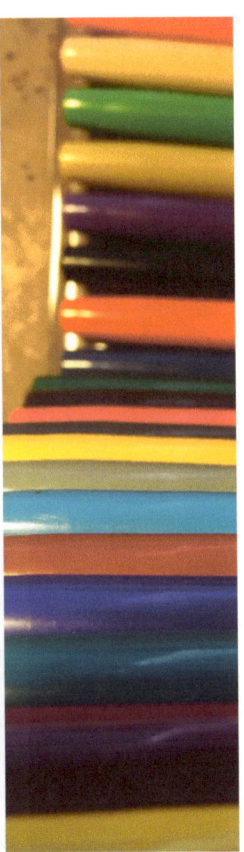

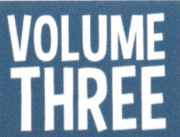

VOLUME THREE

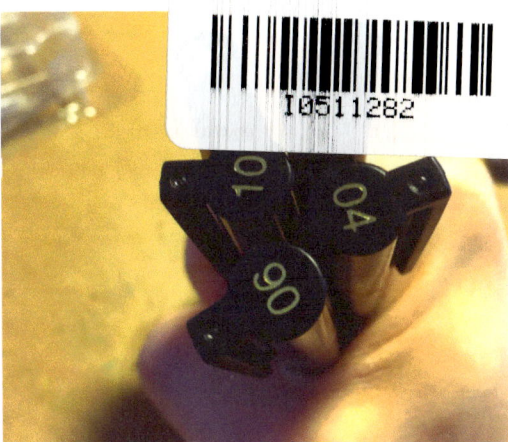

ART BY MARK

Mark Mariano

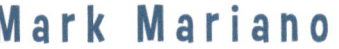

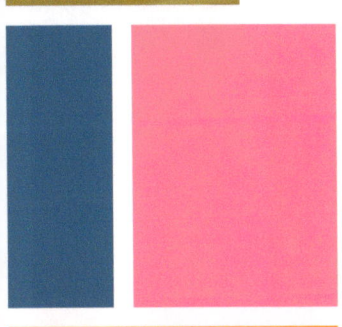

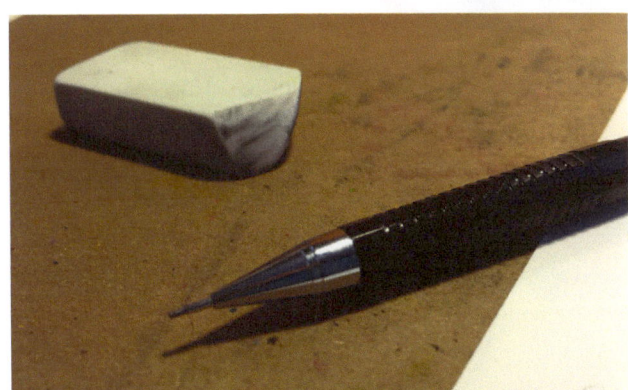

First Edition, September 2015
ISBN 978-1514648650

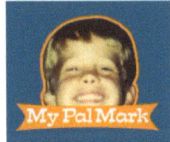

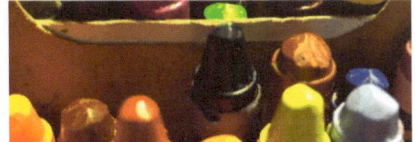

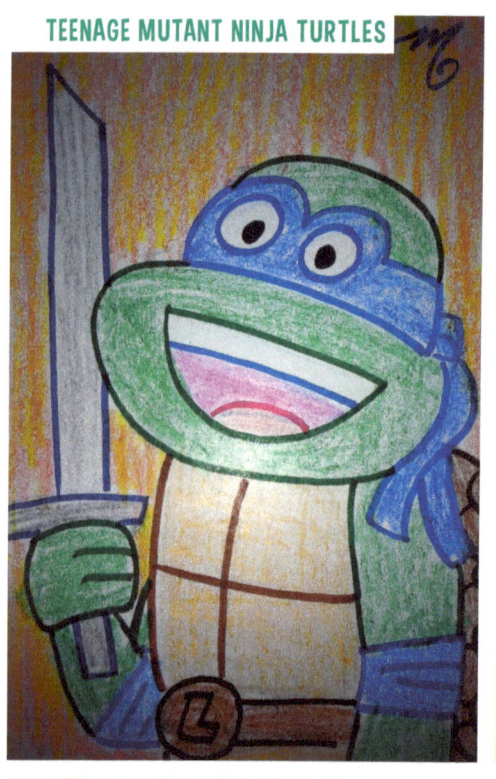

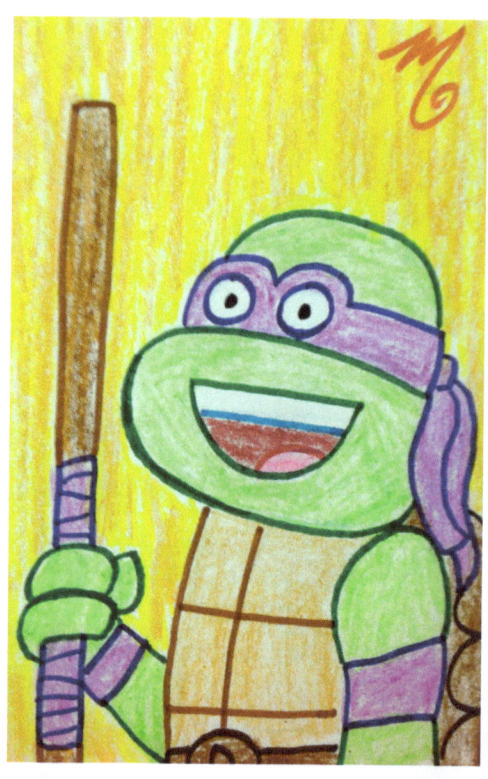

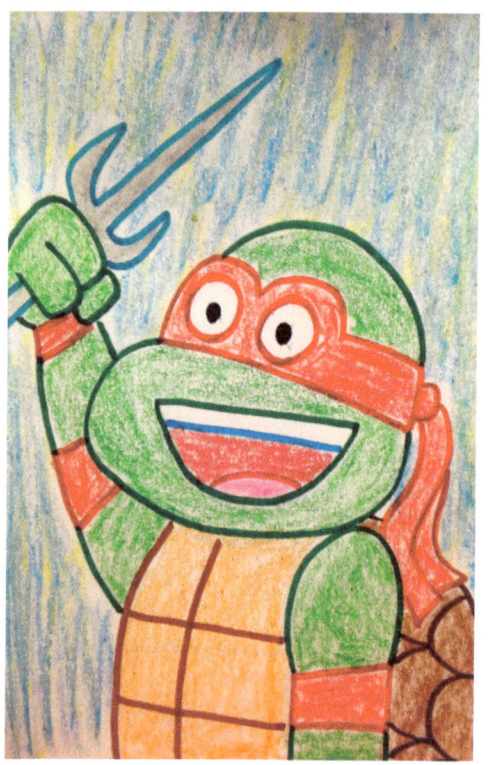

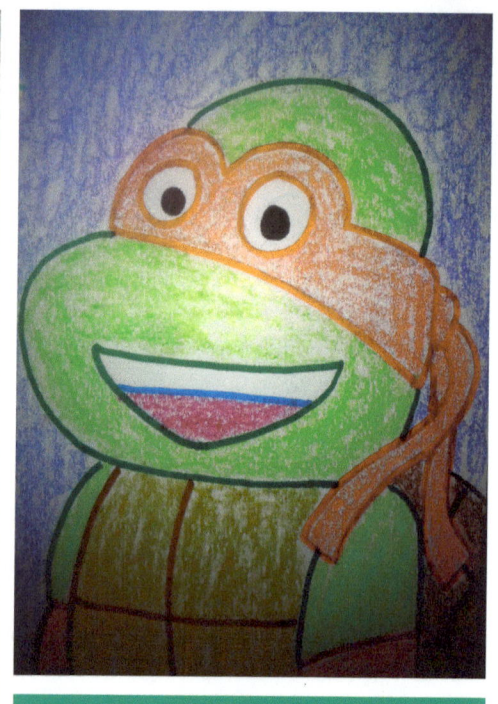

Leonardo, Donatello, Raphael, Michelangelo

The Fantastic Four as kids: The Thing, Human Torch, Sue Storm, Reed Richards

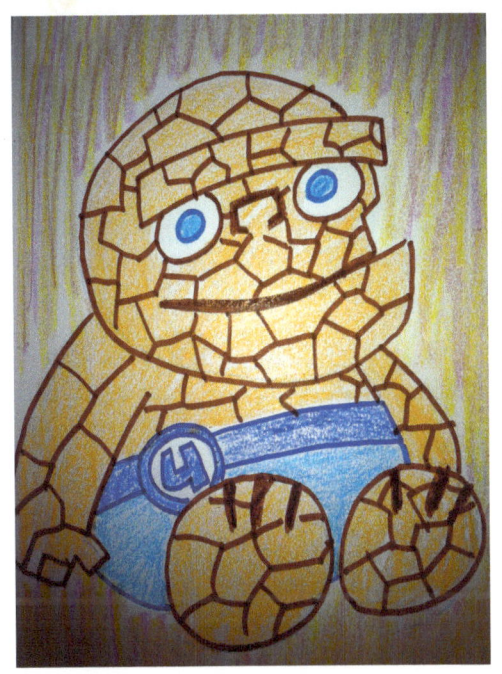

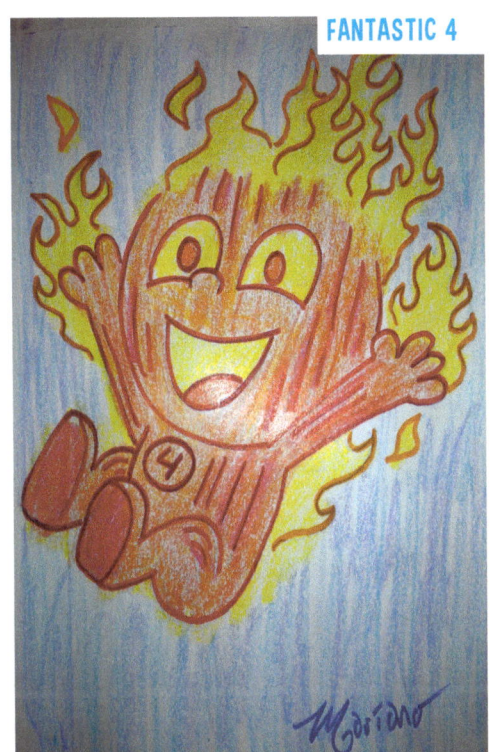

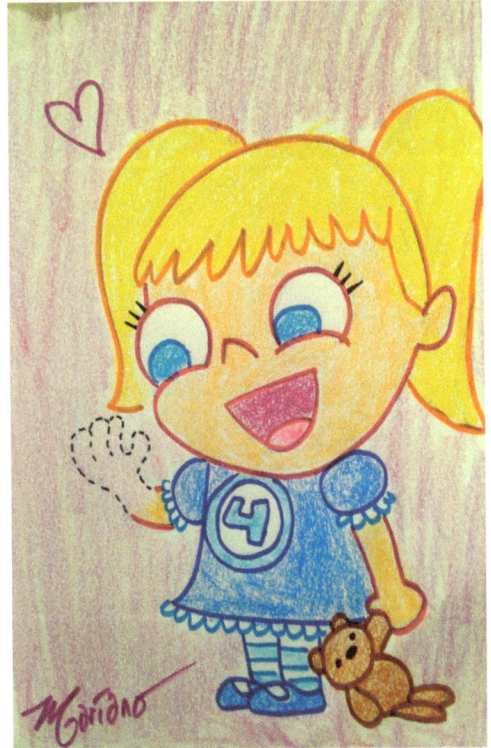

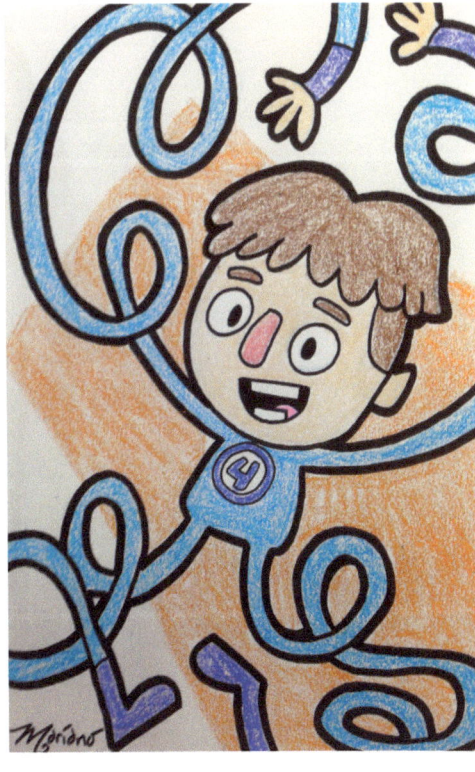

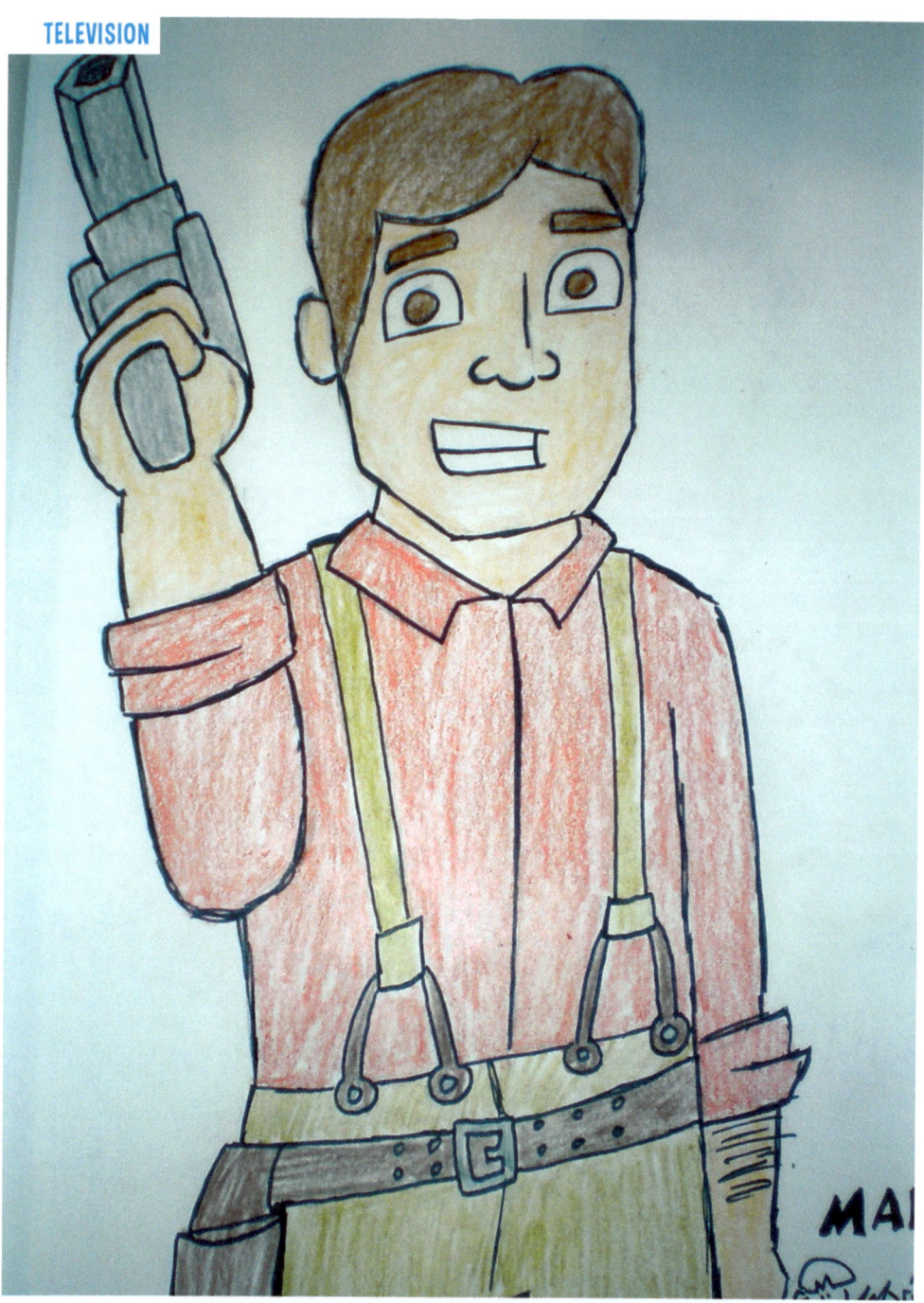

MA

THIS PAGE: Captain Mal Reynolds

OTHER PAGE: Day Man, Larry David, The Hound, Magellan, Bear in the Big Blue House

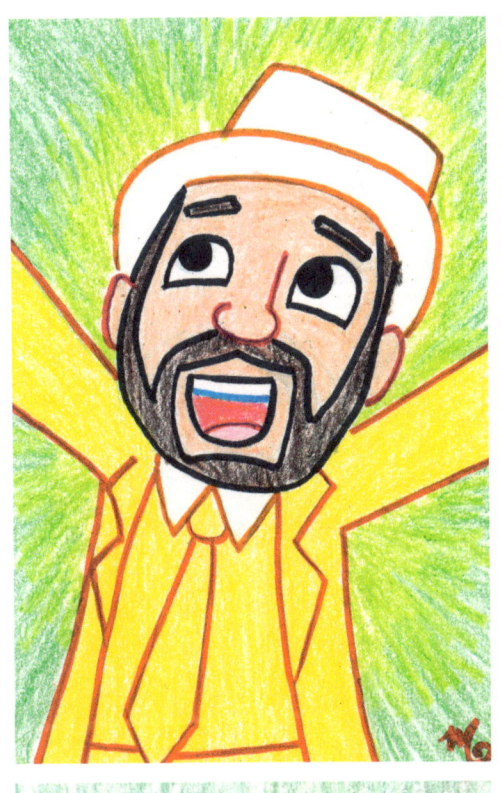
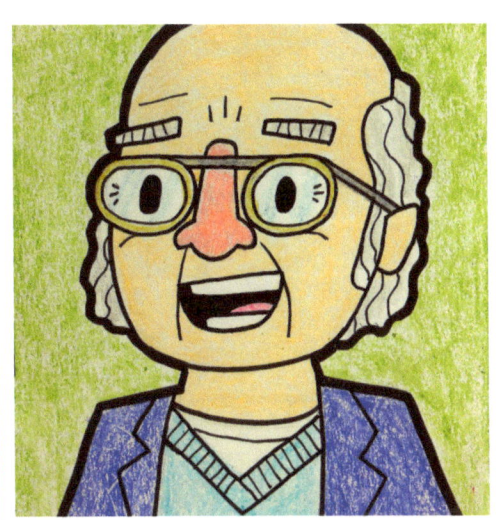
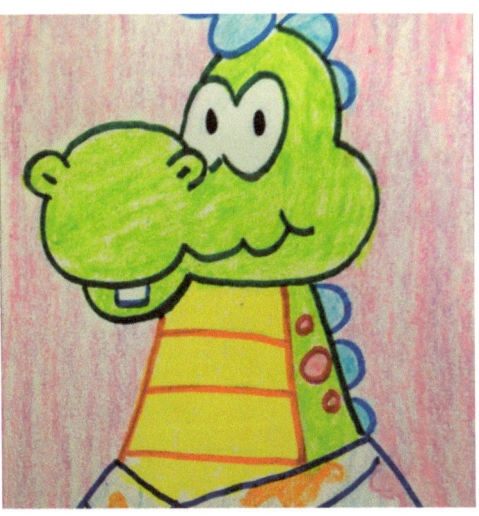
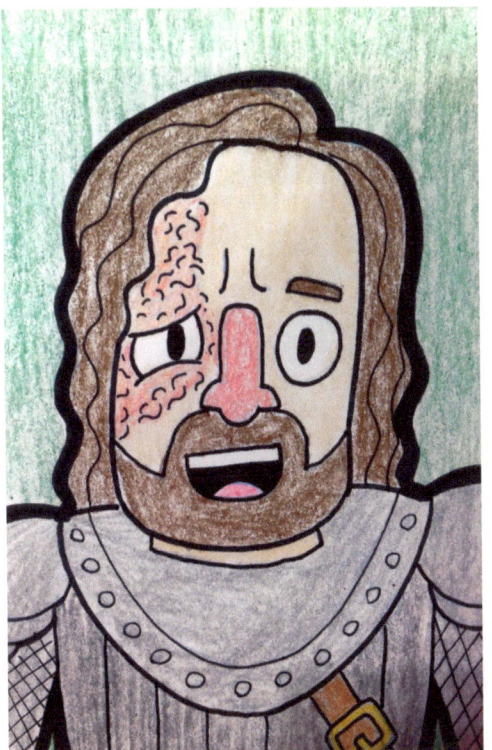
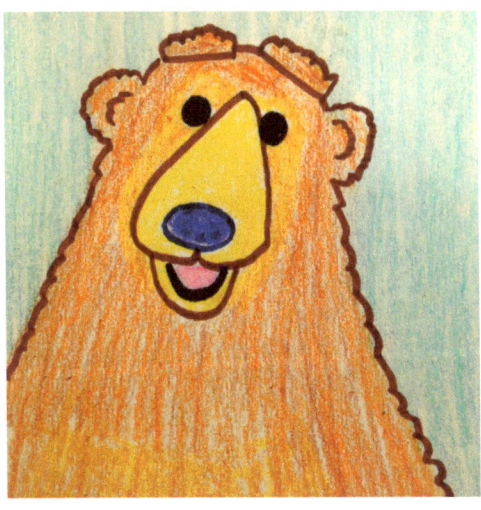

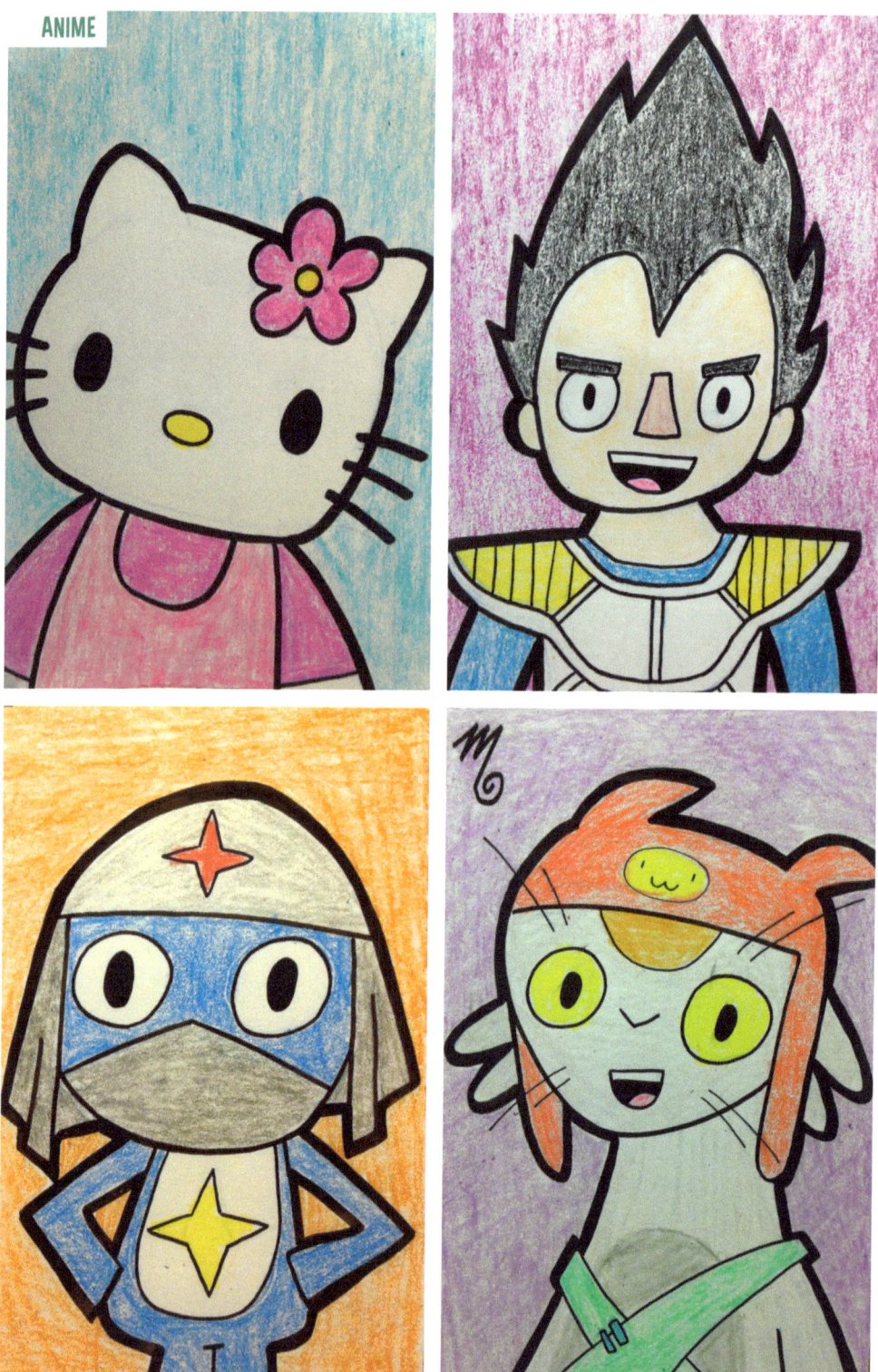

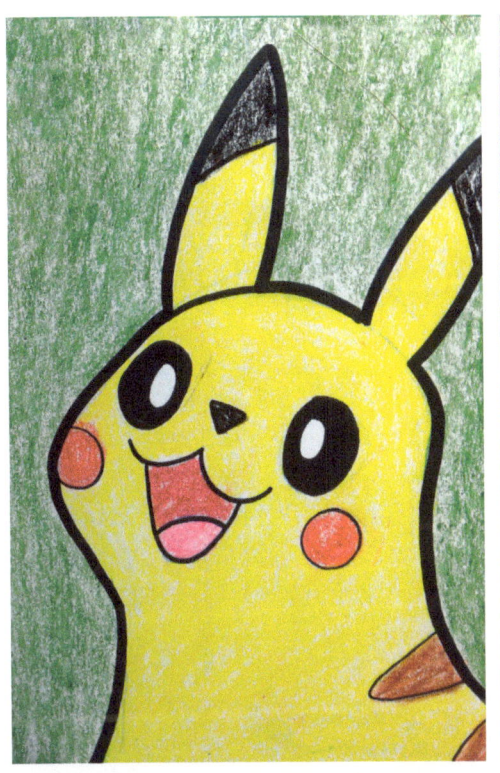

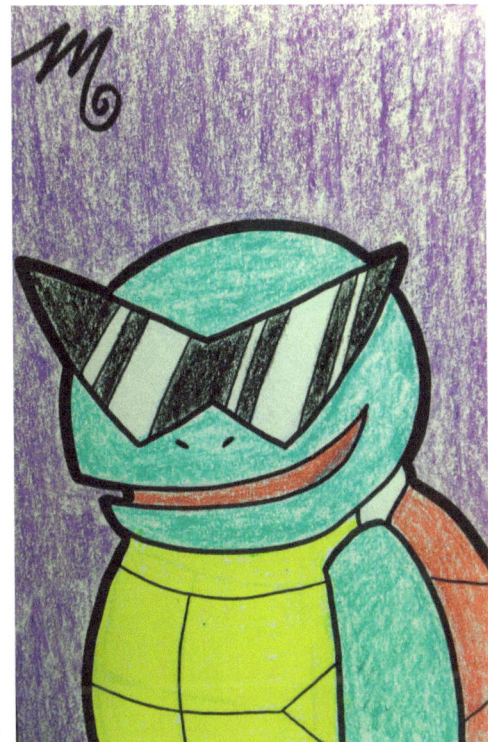

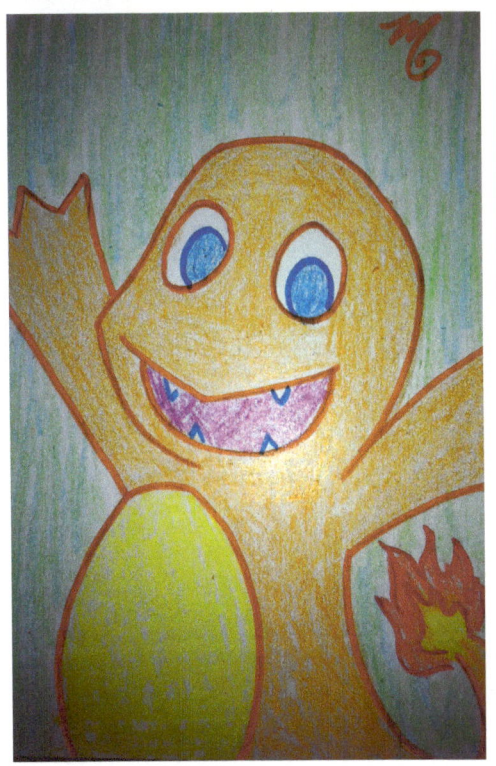

OTHER PAGE:
Hello Kitty
Vegeta
Dororo Keroro
Meow

THIS PAGE:
Pikachu
Squirtle
Charmander

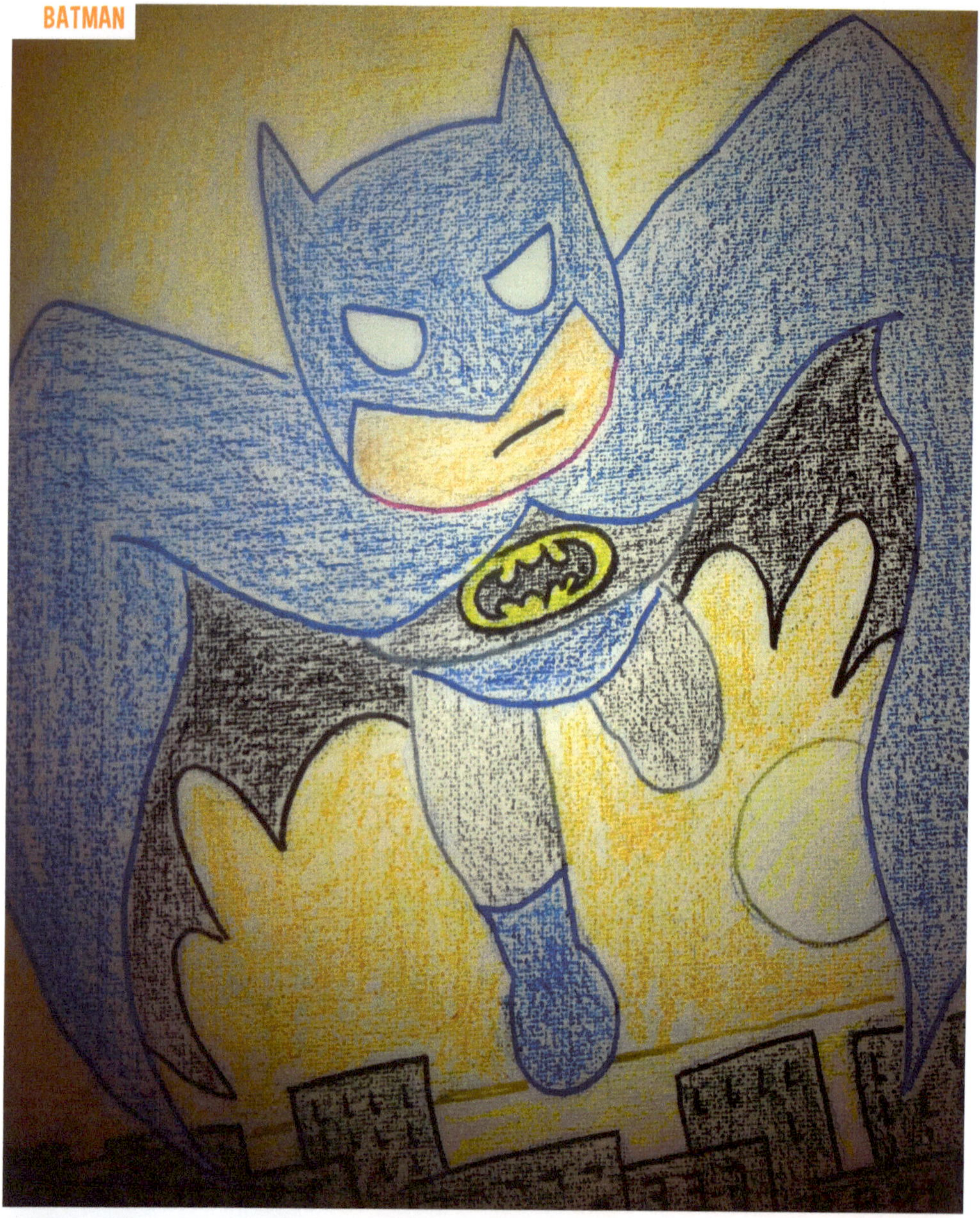

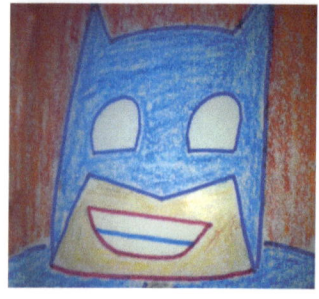

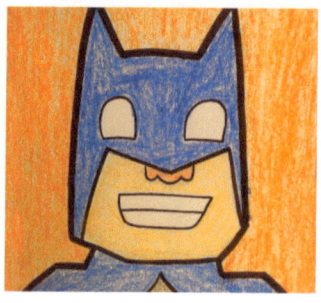

THIS PAGE:
A few versions of Batman

OTHER PAGE:
Nightwing, Joker,
Catwoman with Mark's
cats, Mertle & Yoshi,
BatJoke (mash-up)

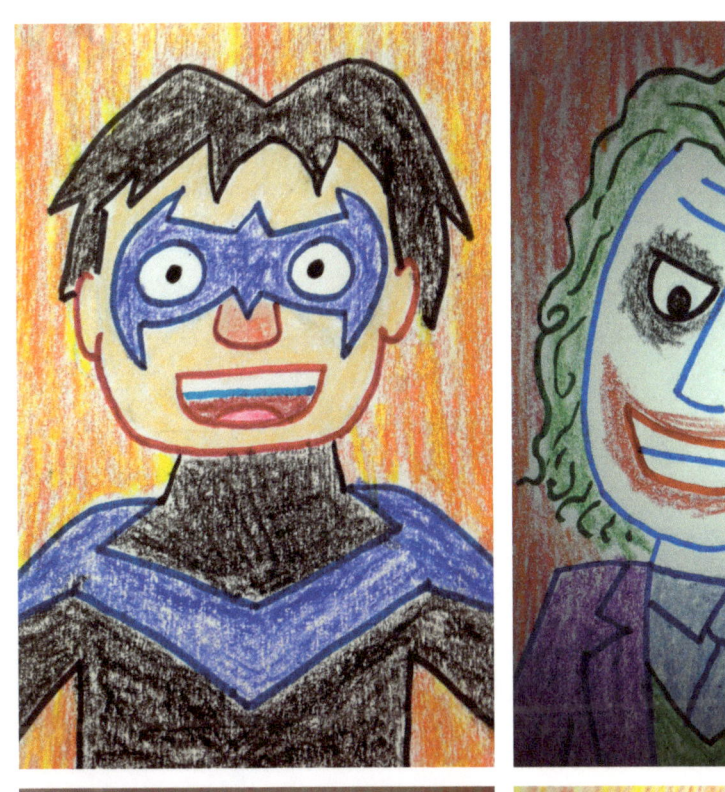
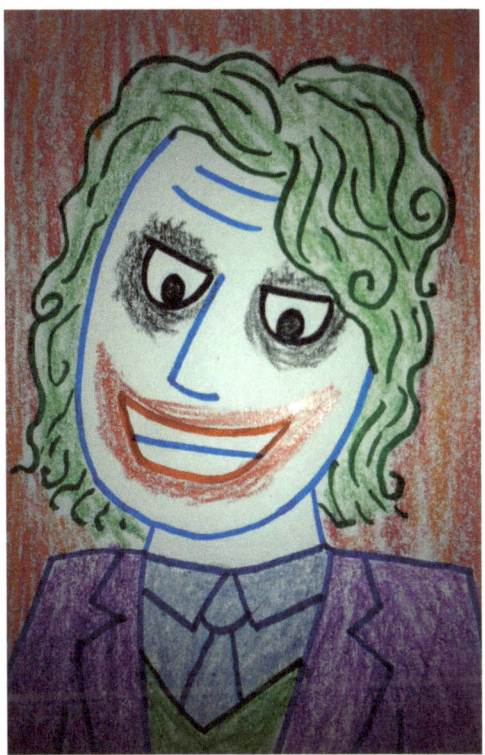
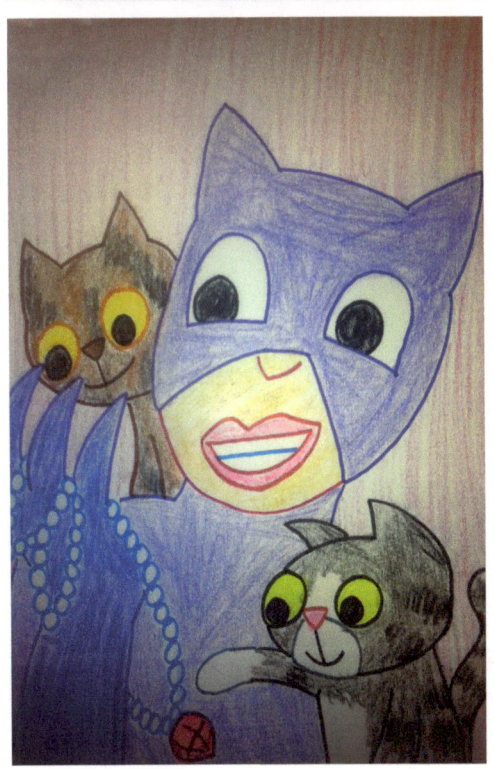
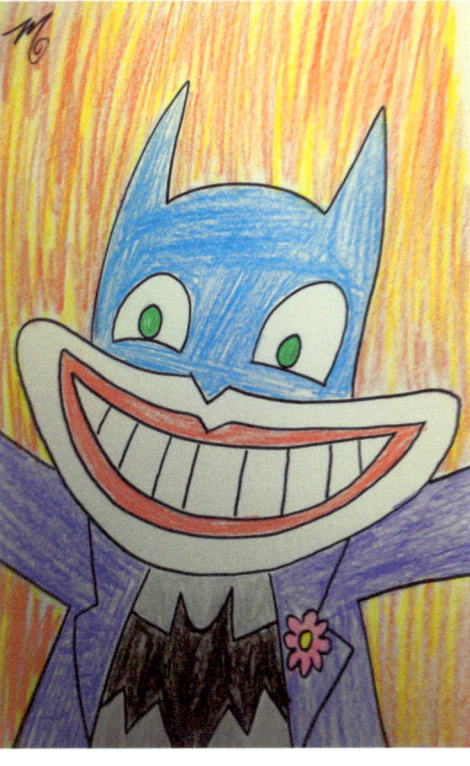

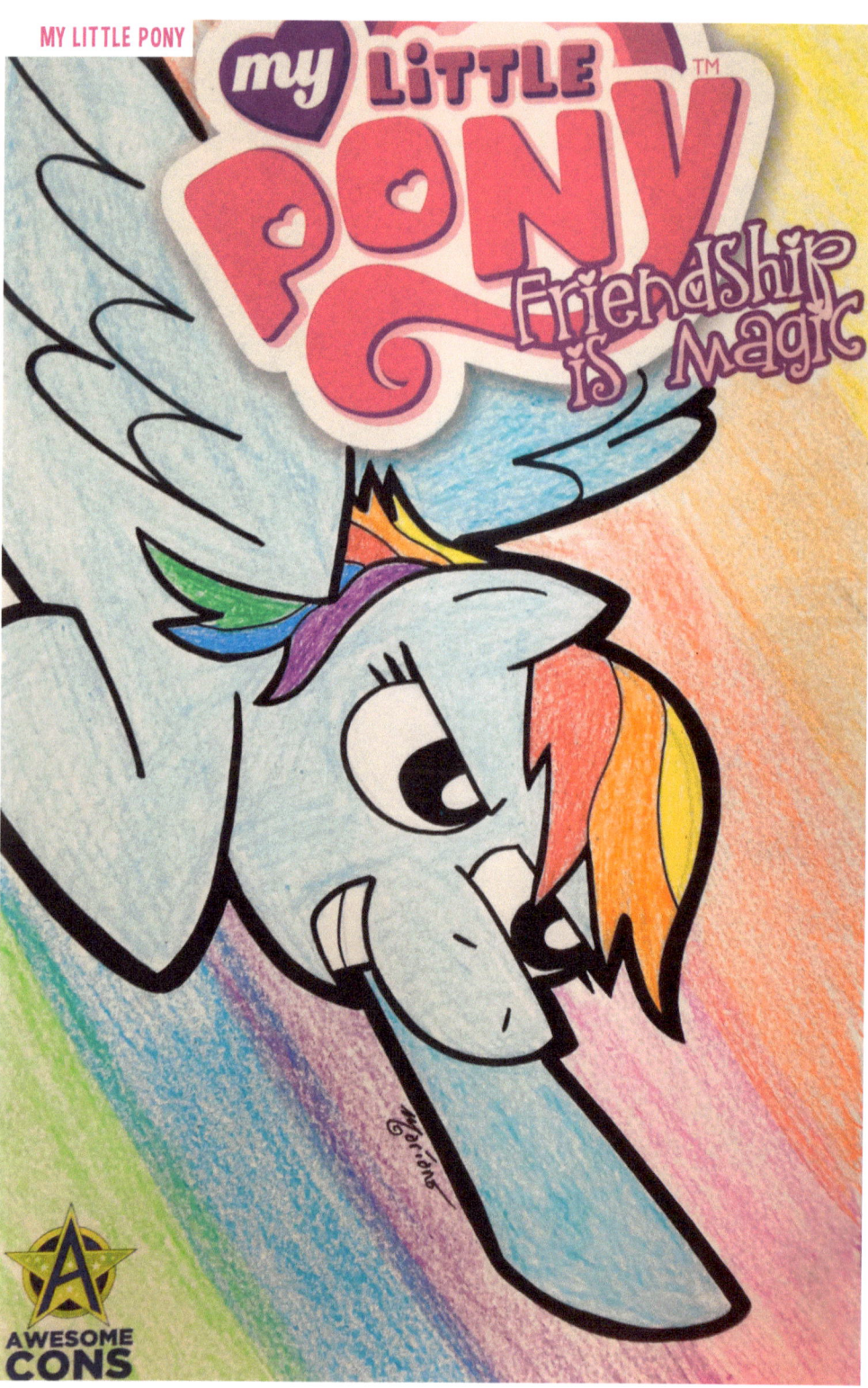

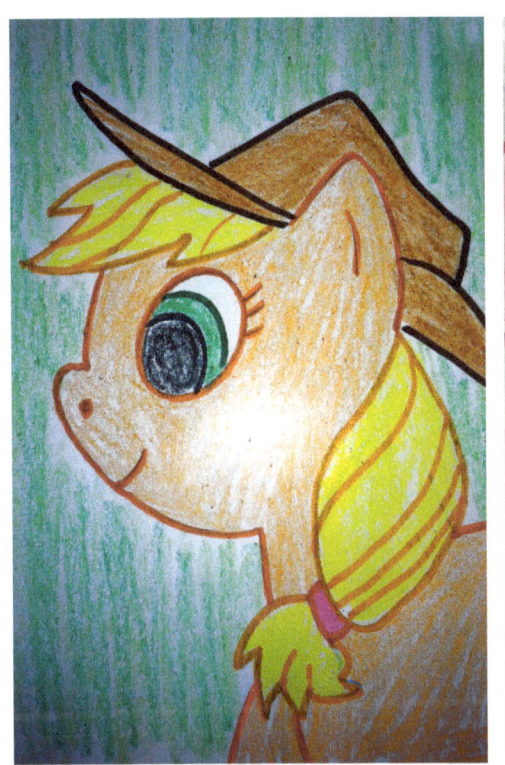
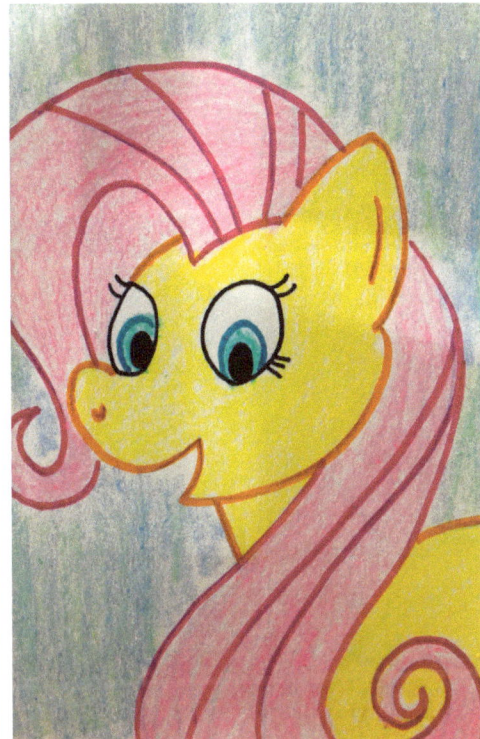
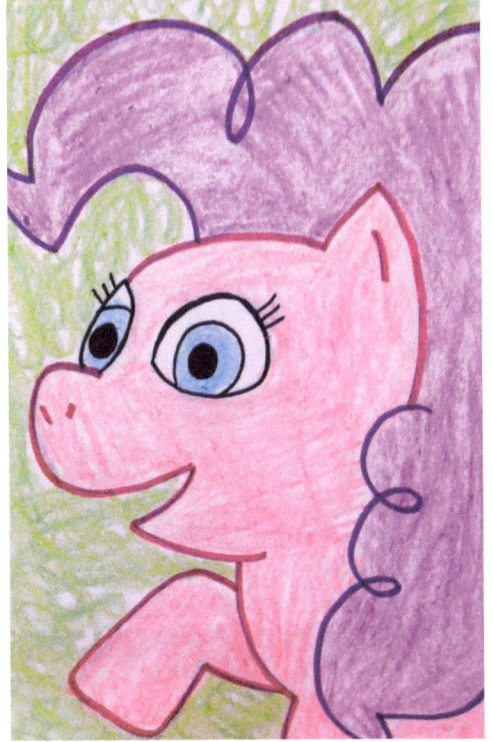
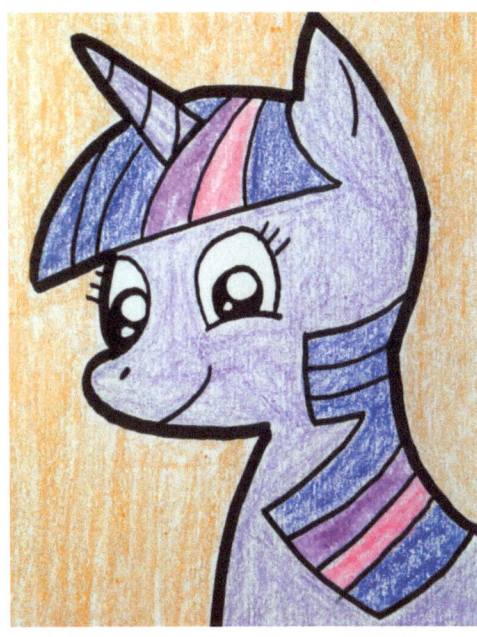

OTHER PAGE: Rainbow Dash Sketch Cover
THIS PAGE: Applejack, Fluttershy,
Pinkie Pie, Twighlight Sparkle

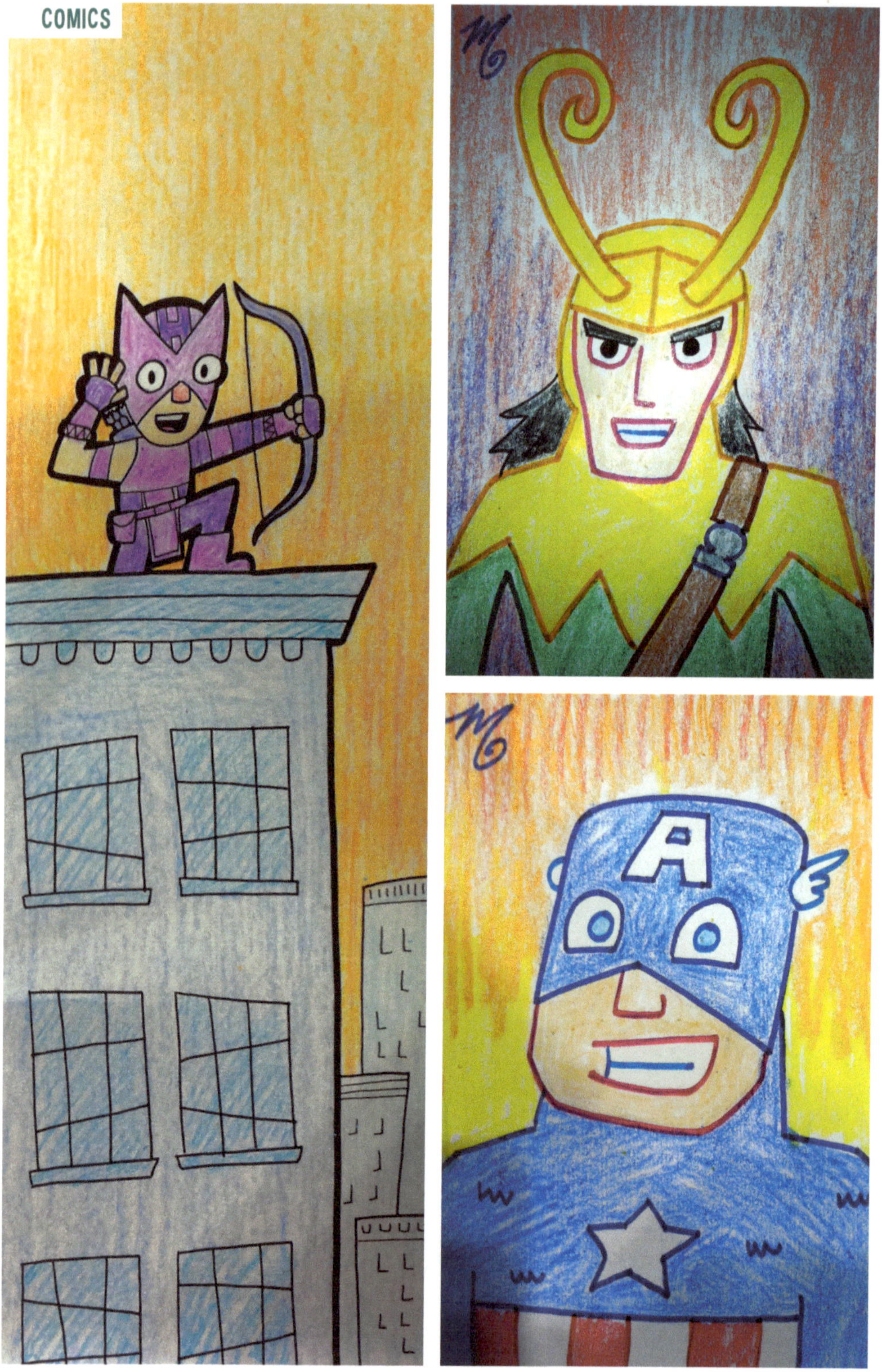

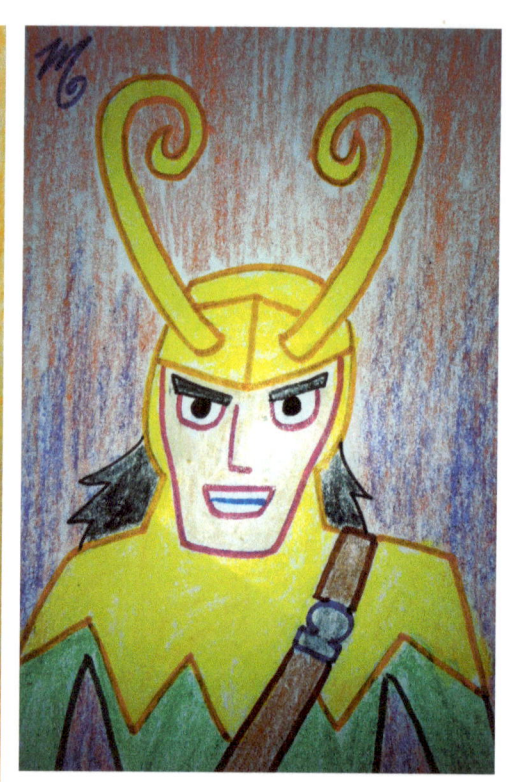

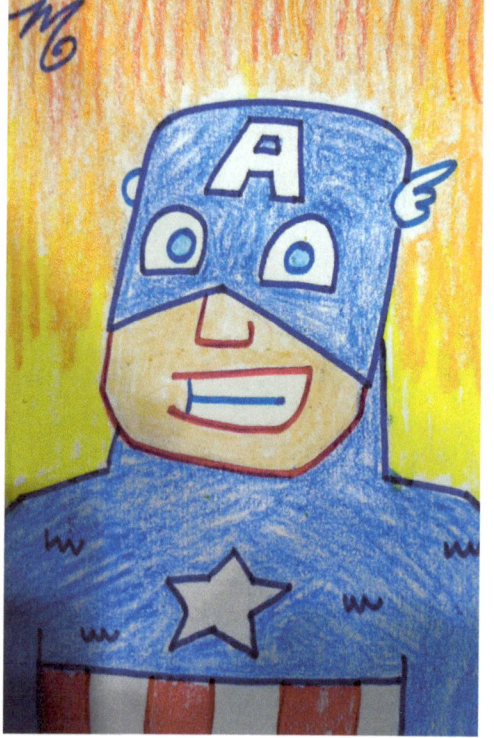

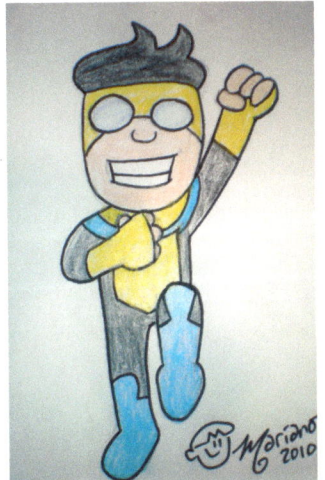

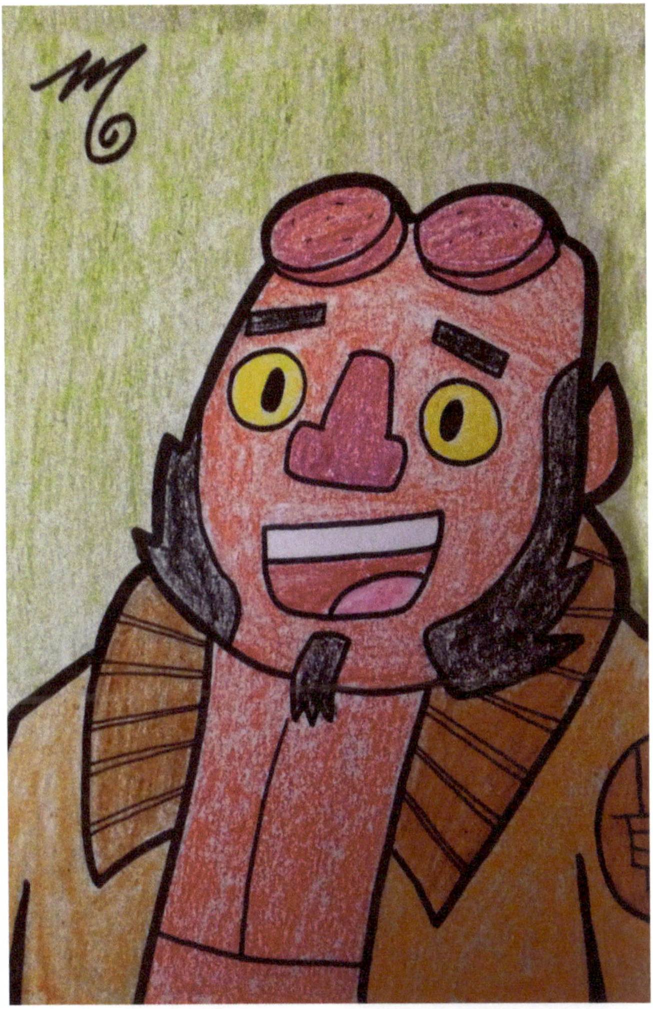

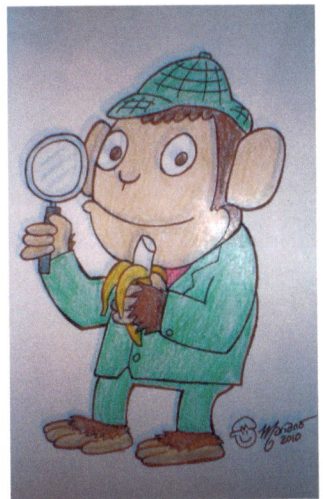

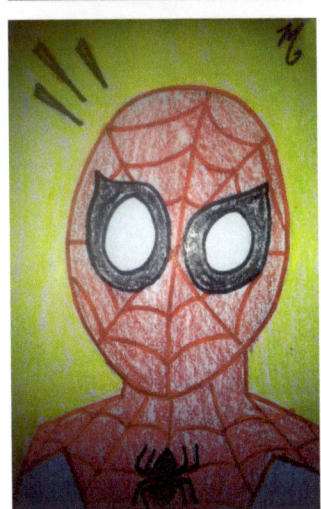

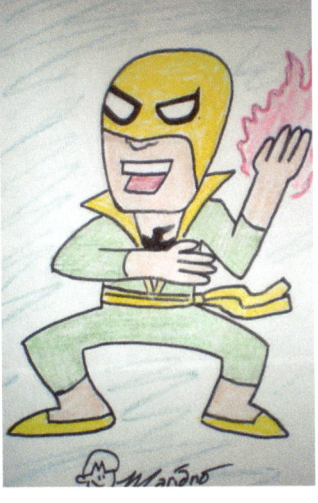

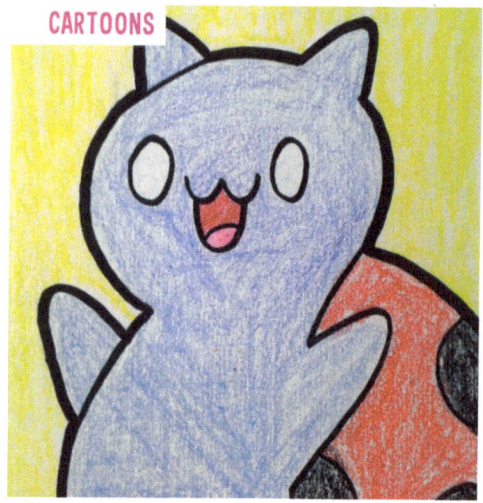

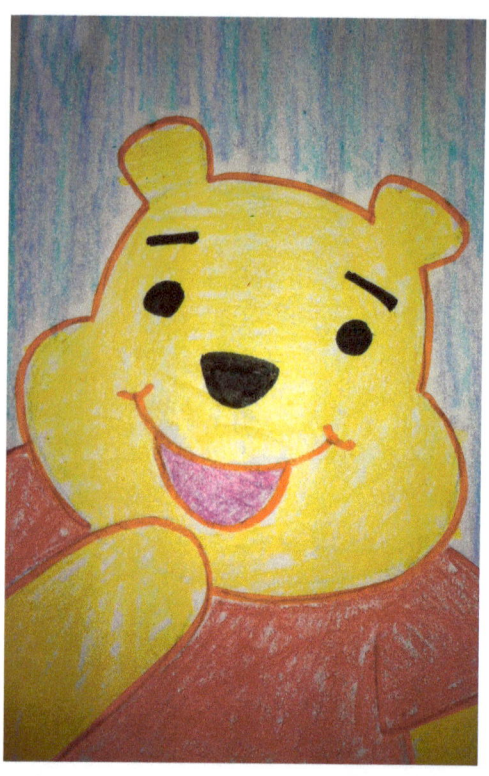

THIS PAGE:
Cat Bug
Winnie the Pooh
Poof
Eduardo

OTHER PAGE:
Cap'n K'nuckles
Strong Bad
Space Ghost
Steven Universe
Aquaman

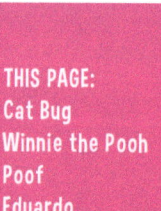

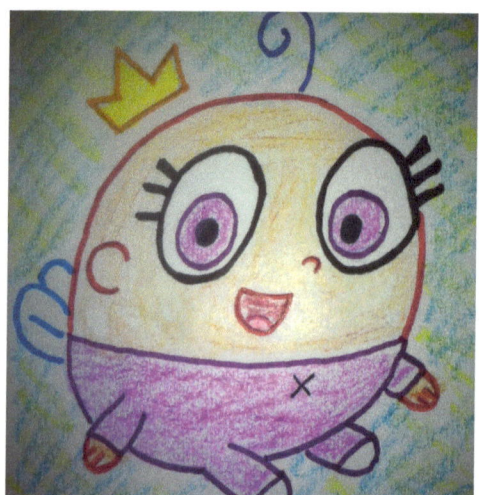

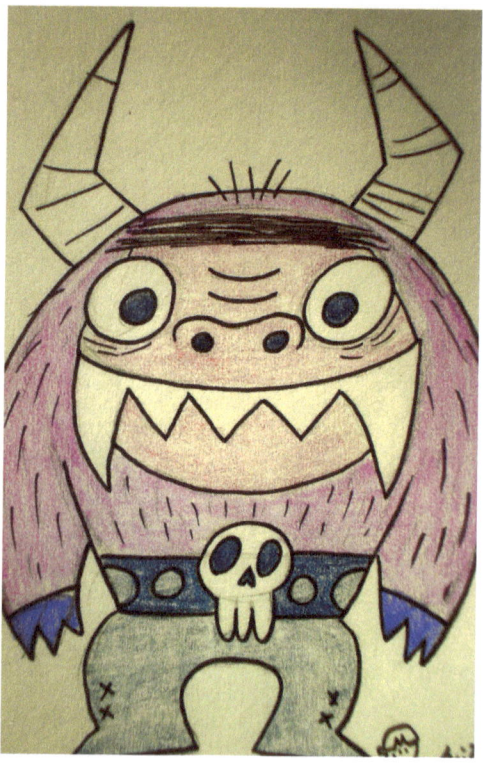

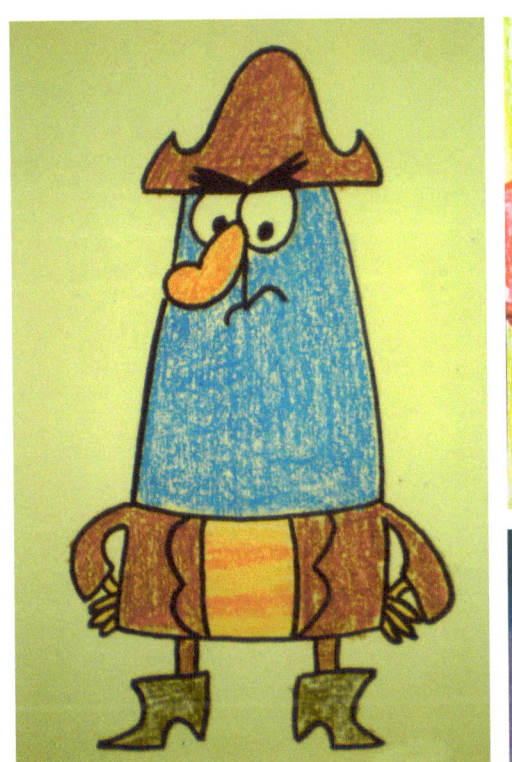

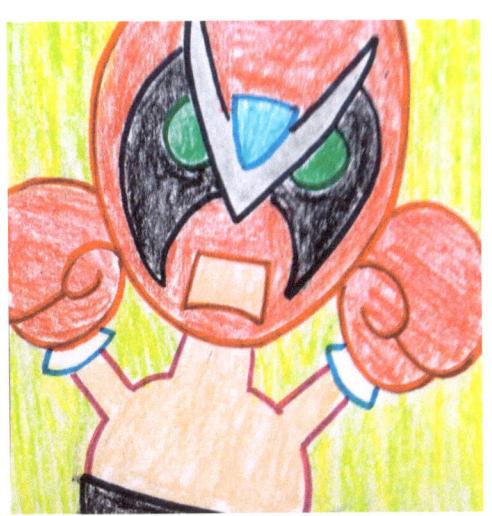

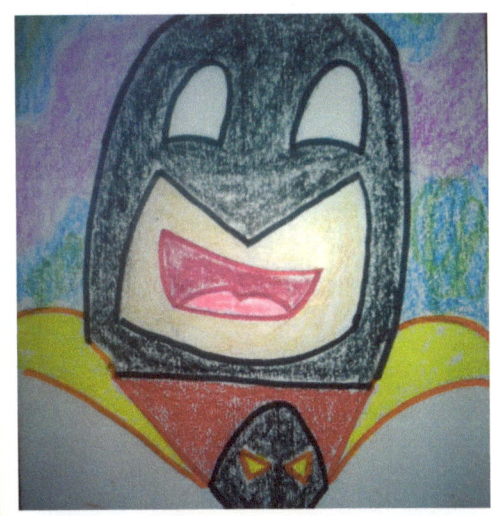

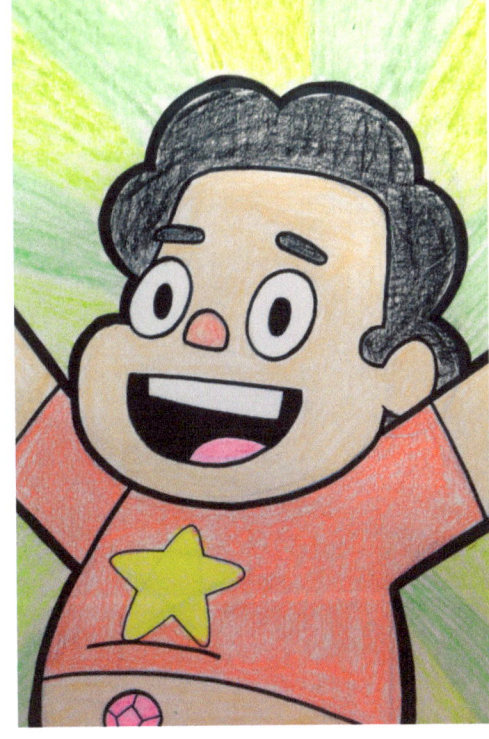

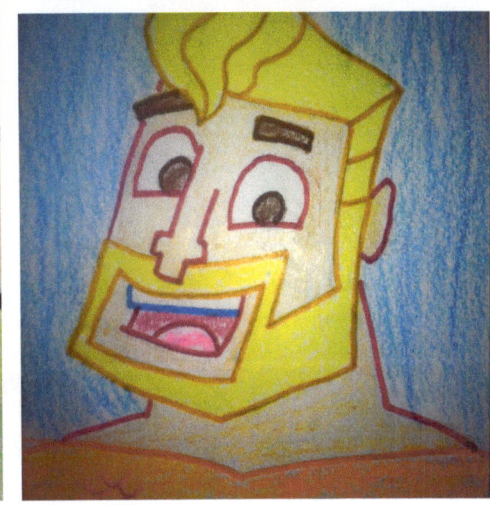

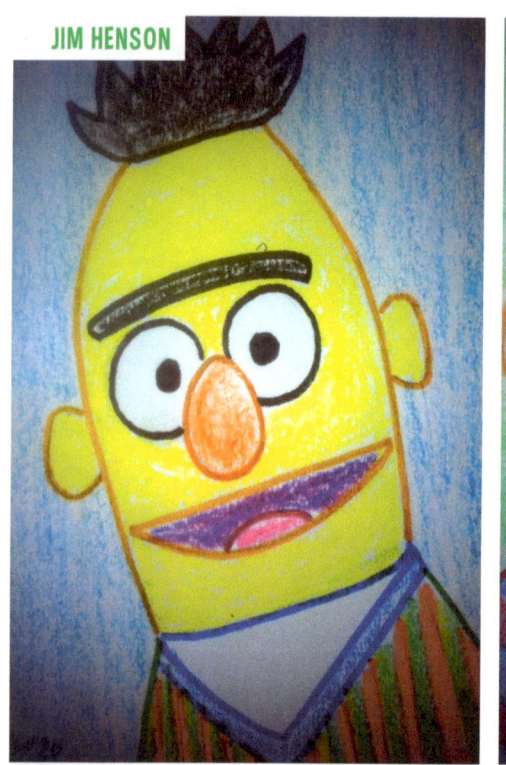

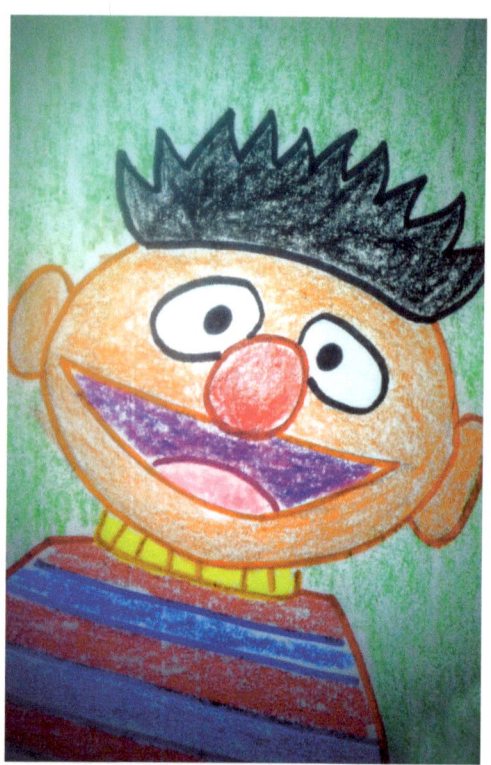

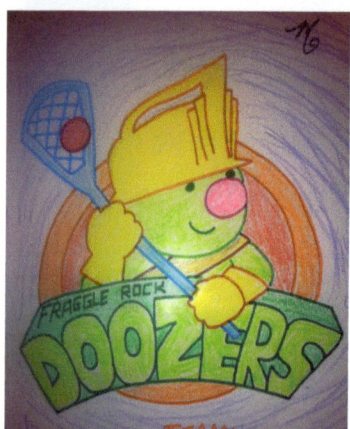

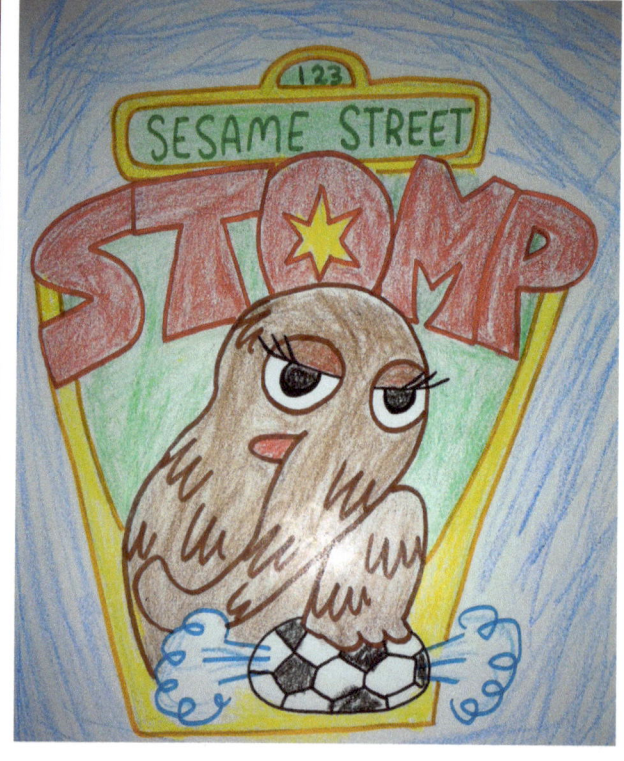

THIS PAGE:
Bert, Ernie
Doozers Team Logo,
Stomp Team Logo,

OTHER PAGE:
Elmo, Cookie Monster,
BatElmo, The Count

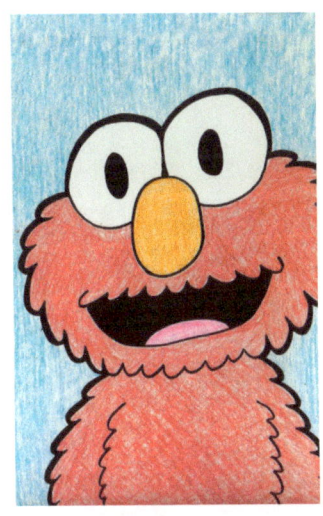
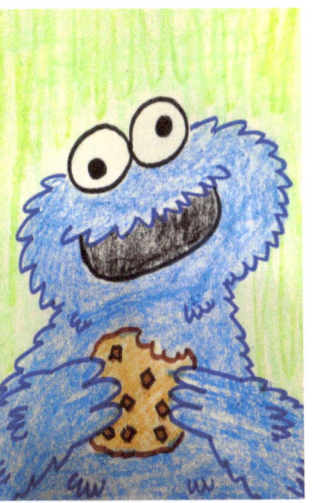
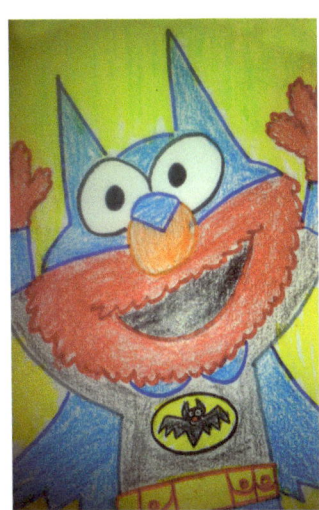

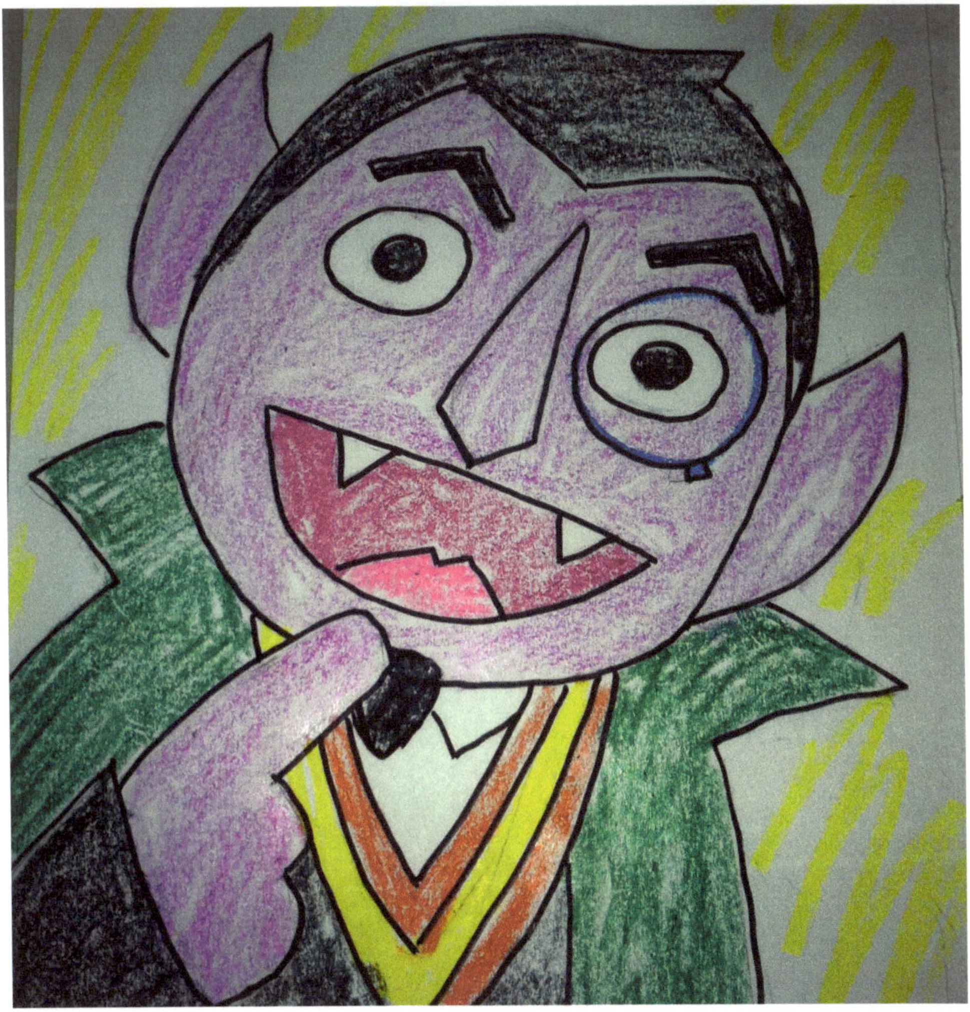

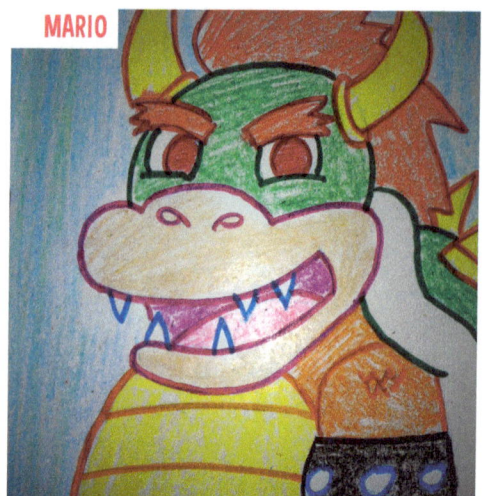

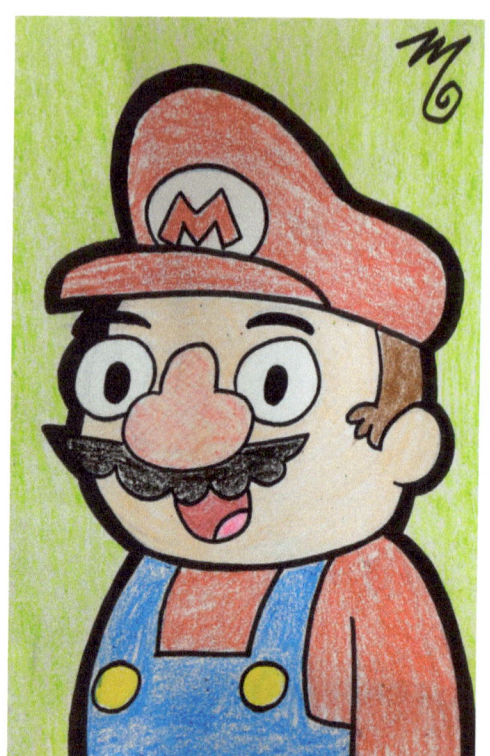

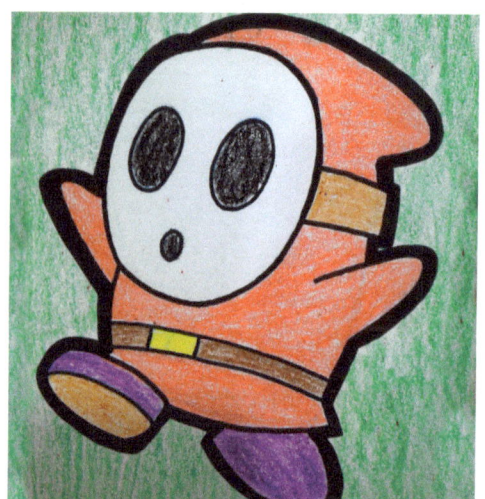

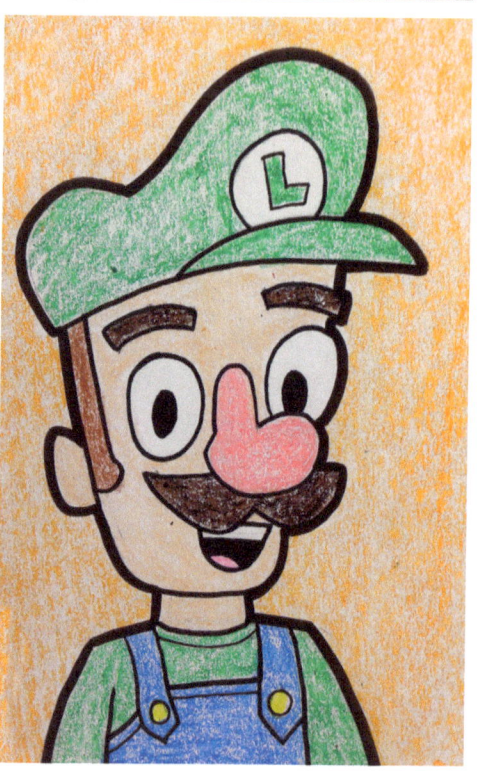

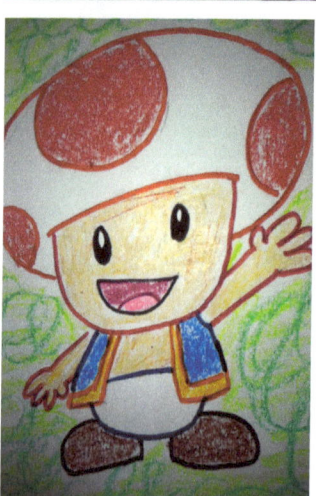

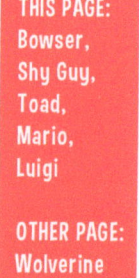

THIS PAGE:
Bowser,
Shy Guy,
Toad,
Mario,
Luigi

OTHER PAGE:
Wolverine
Mario &
Hulk Luigi,
Koopa
Troopa,
Dry Bones

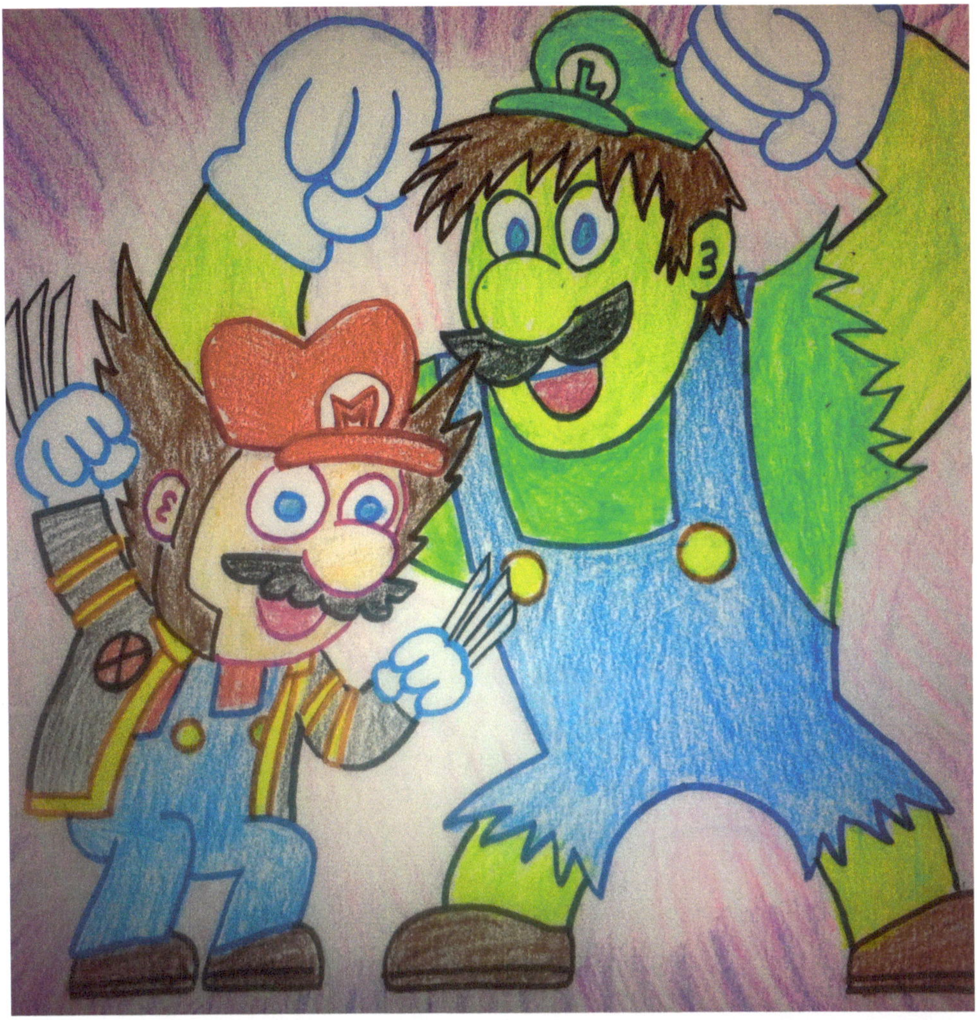

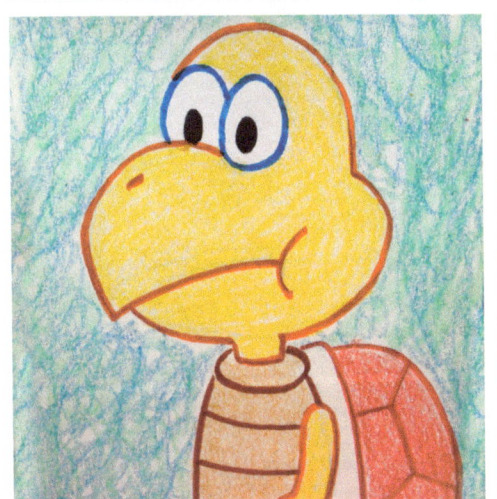
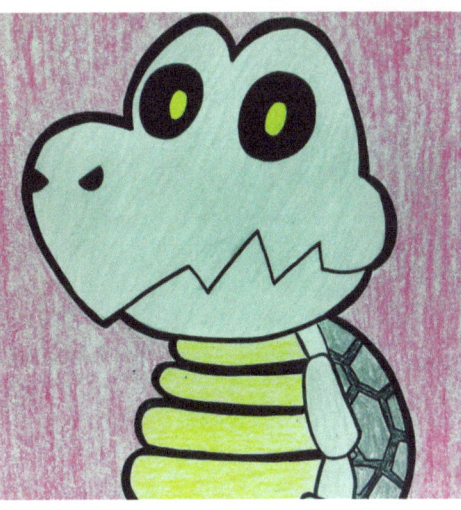

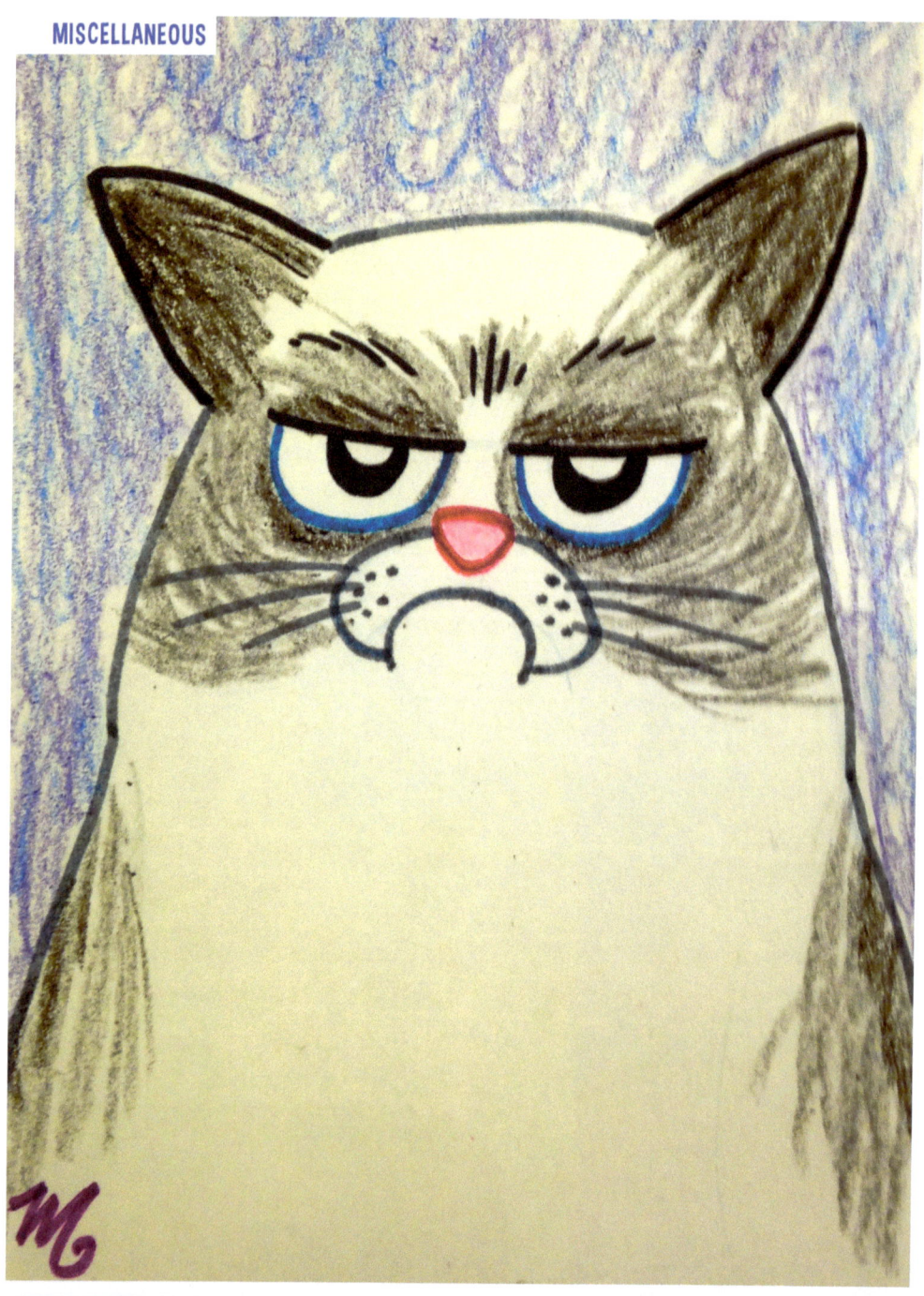

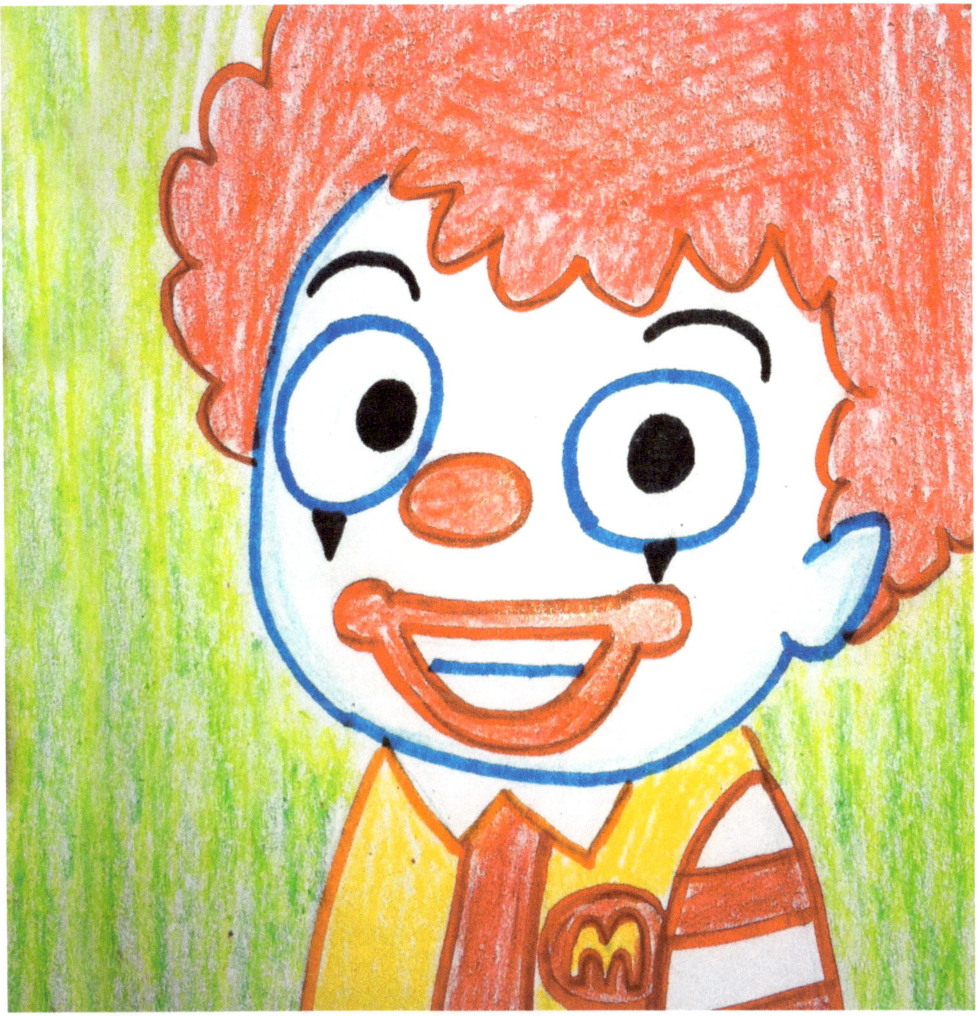

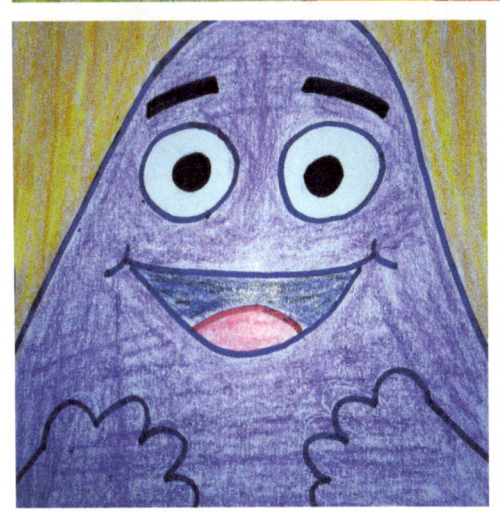
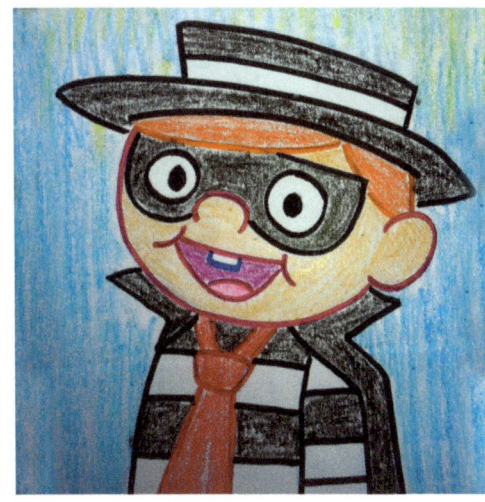

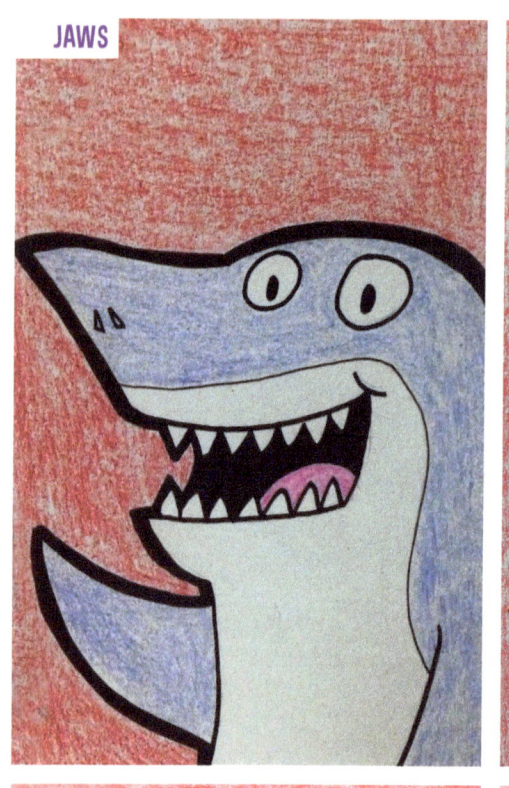
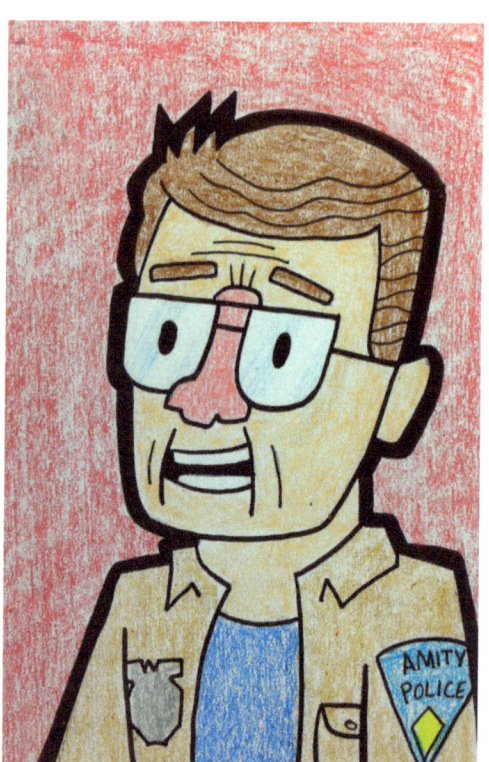
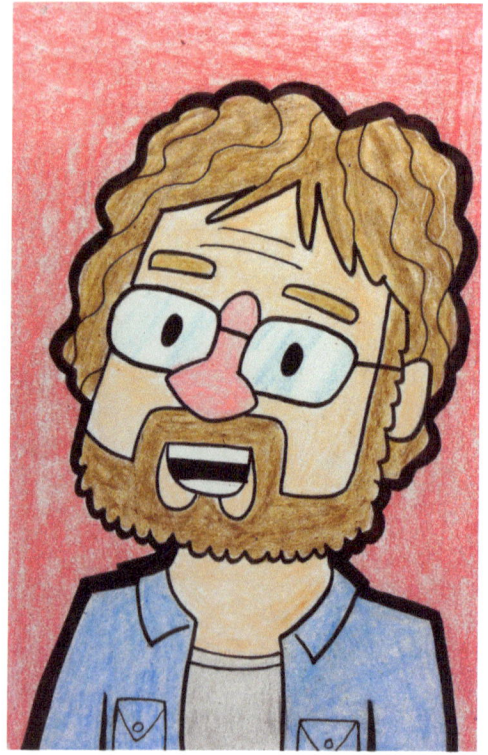
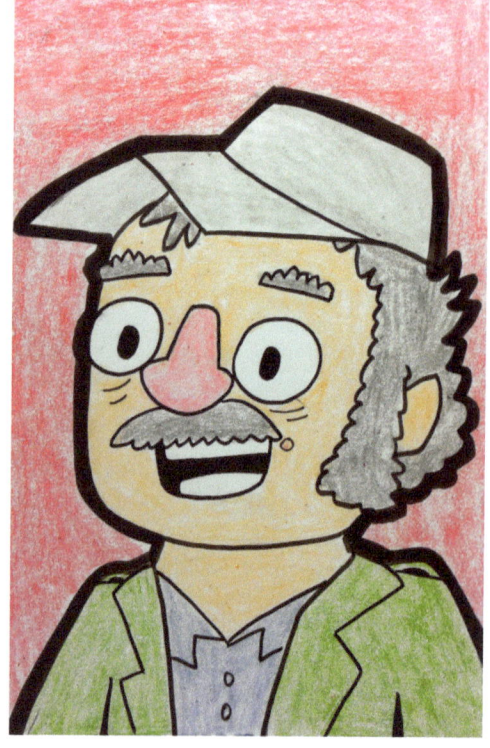

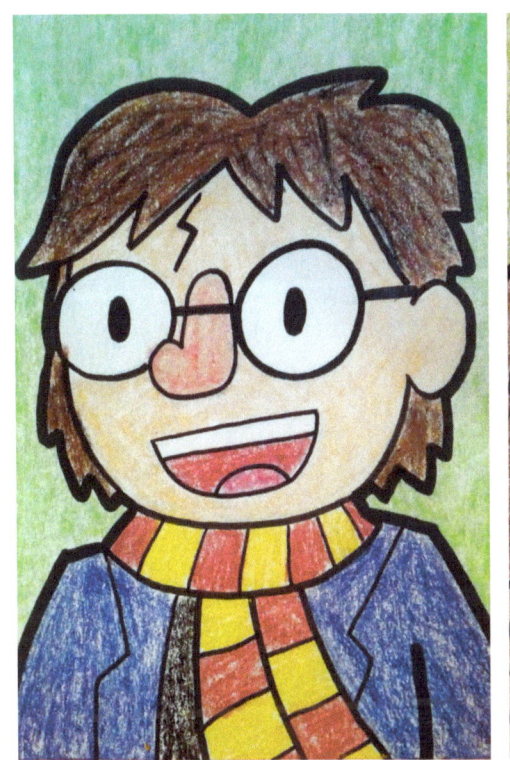

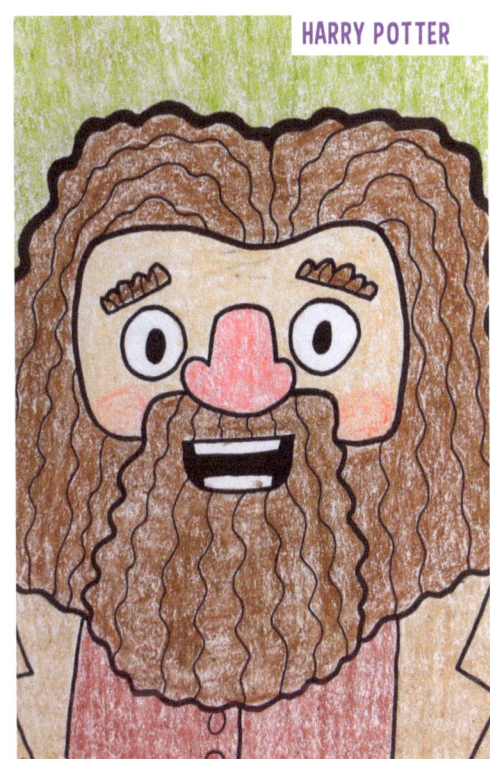

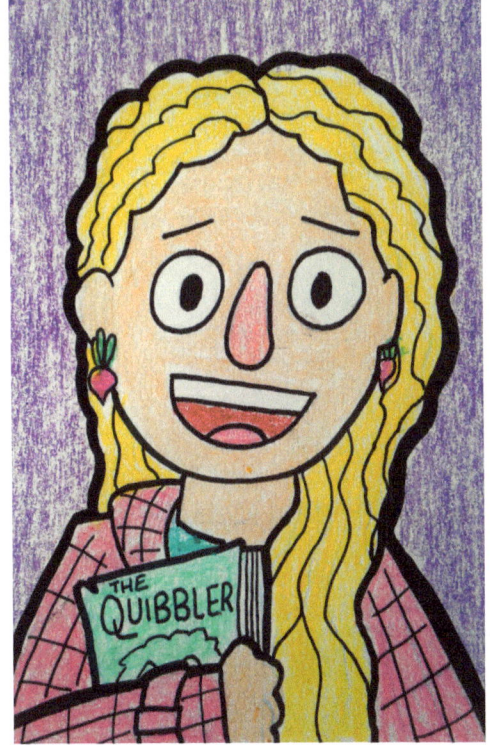

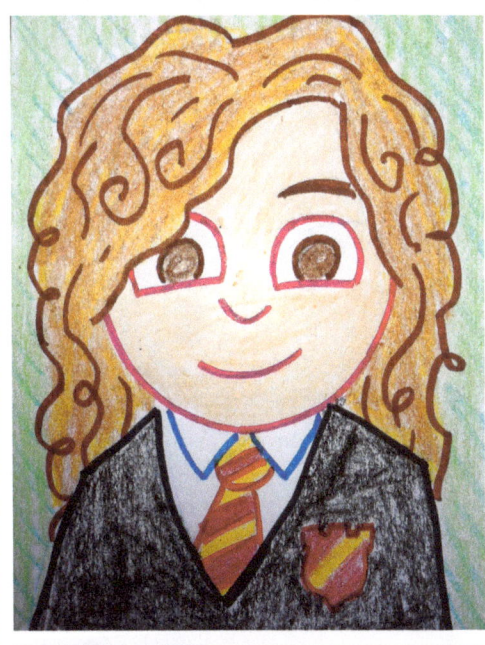

OTHER PAGE: Jaws, Brody, Hooper, Quint
THIS PAGE: Harry Potter, Hagrid,
Luna Lovegood, Hermione Granger

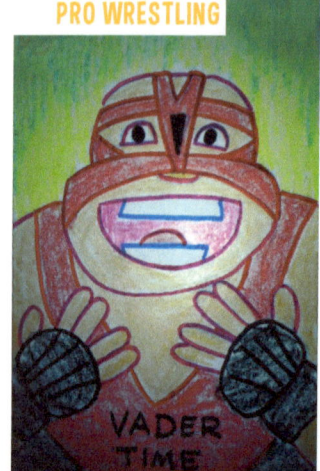

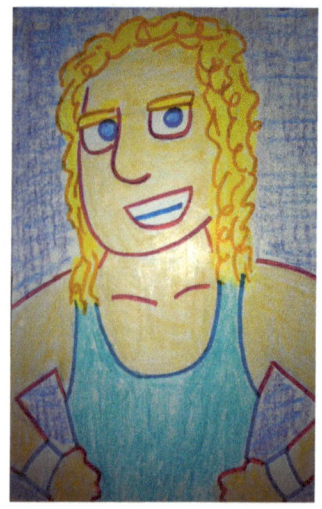

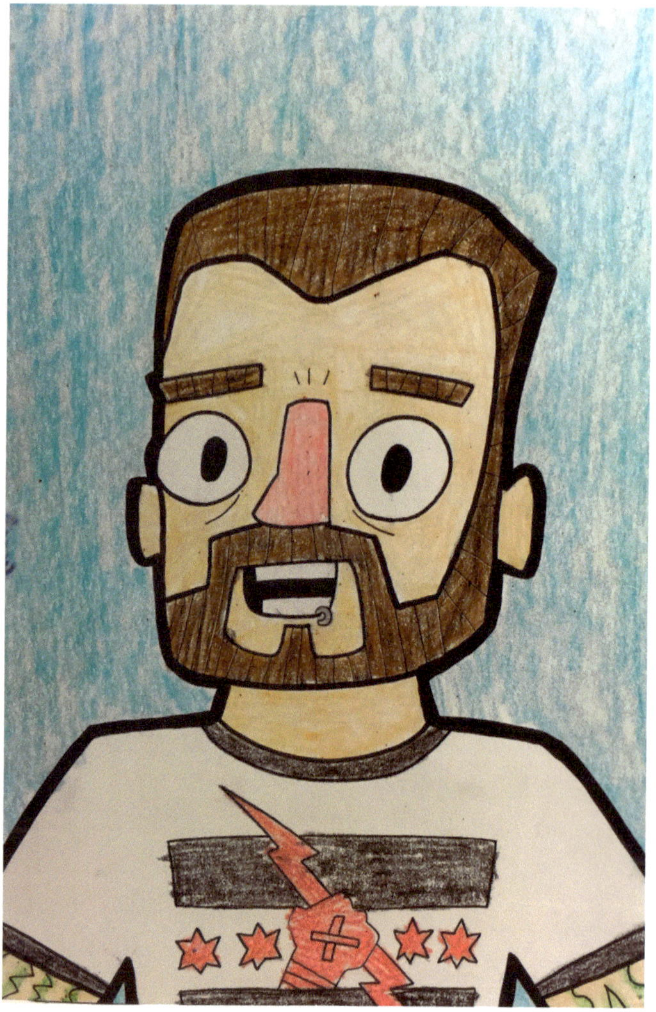

THIS PAGE:
Big Van Vader
Mr. Perfect
CM Punk
Kamala
El Generico

OTHER PAGE:
Daniel Bryan
Bret Hart
Seth Rollins
Hulk Hogan
Goldust
Dolph Ziggler

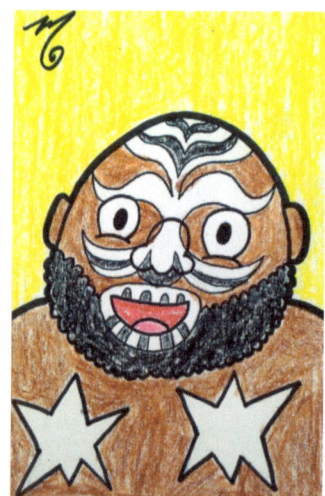

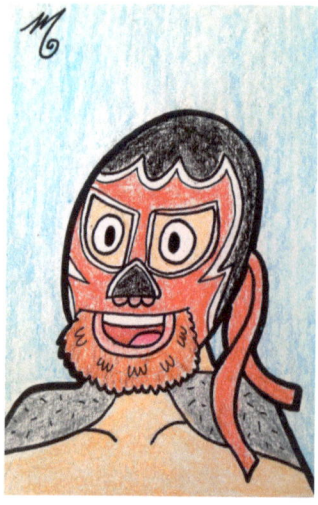

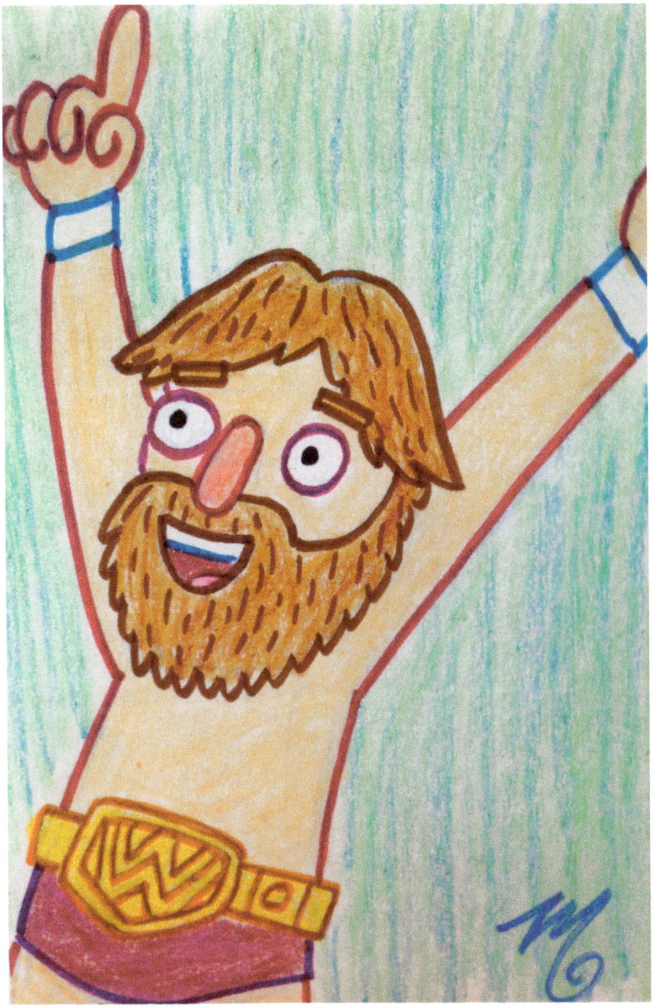

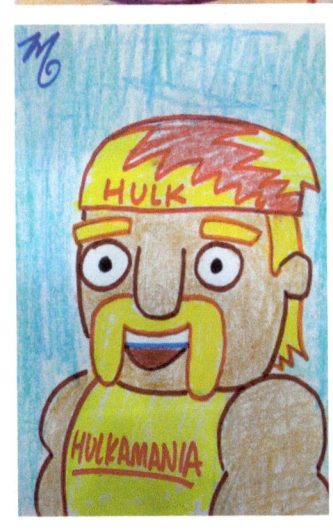
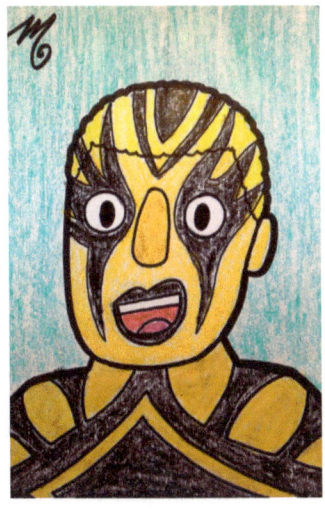
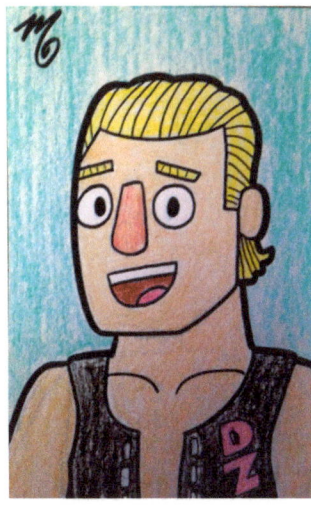
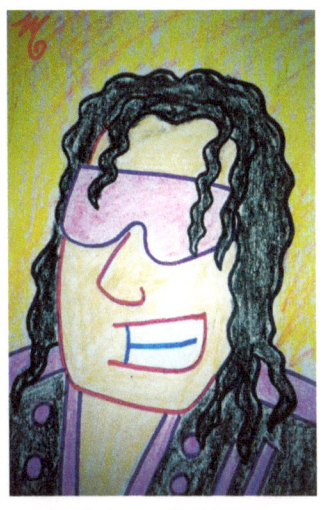
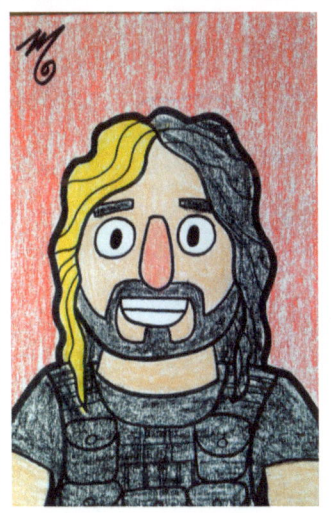

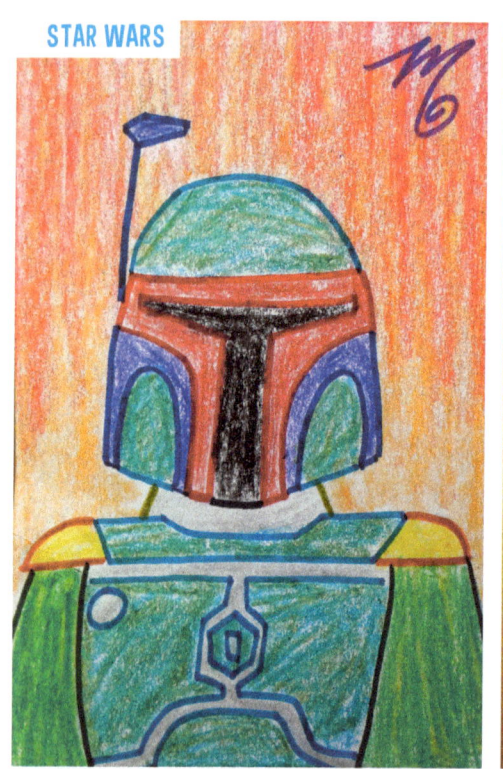

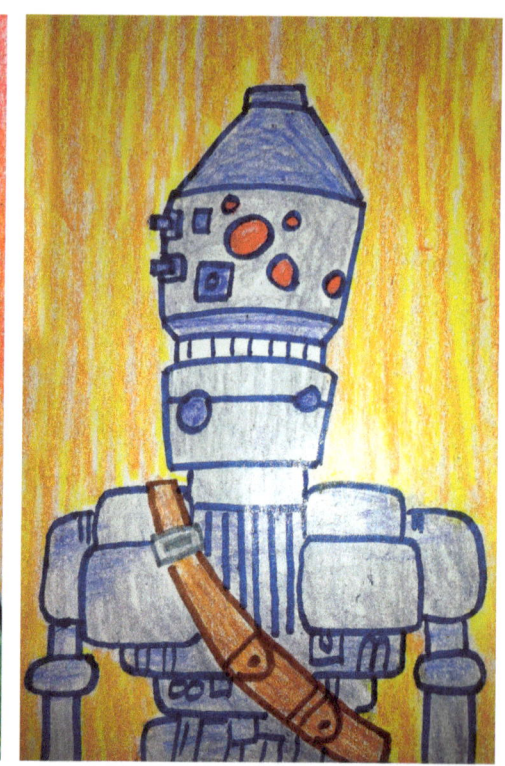

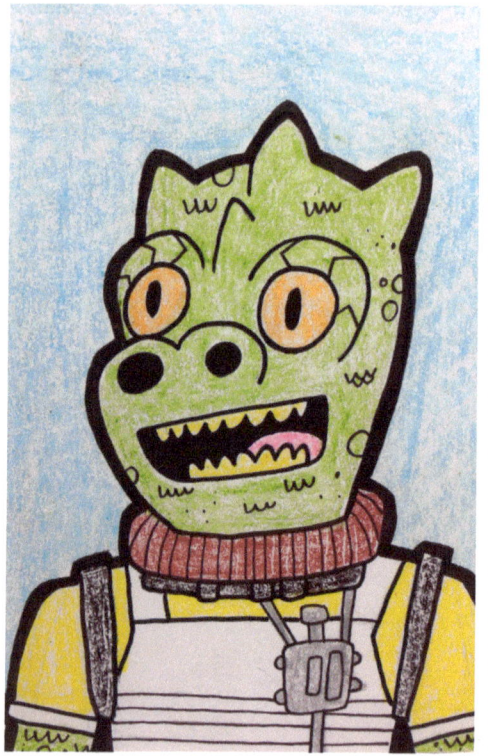

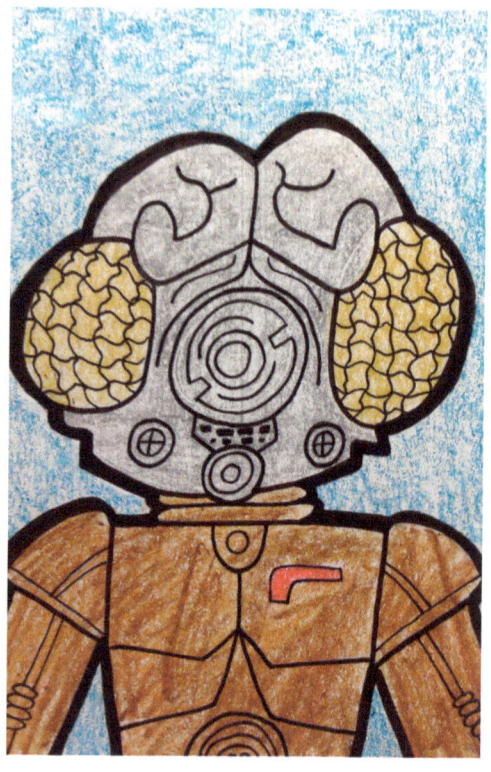

OTHER PAGE:
Boba Fett, IG-88, Bossk, 4-LOM
THIS PAGE:
Zuckuss, Dengar, Ahsoka Tano, Admiral Ackbar

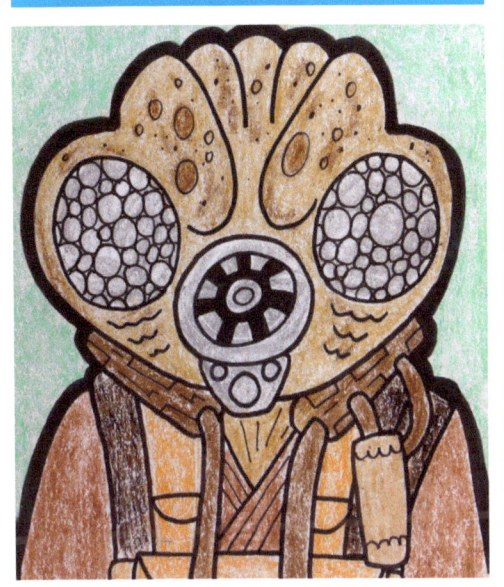

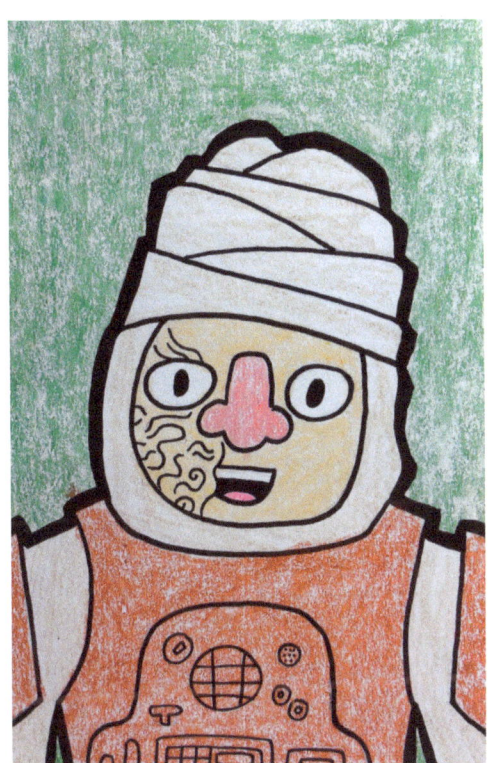

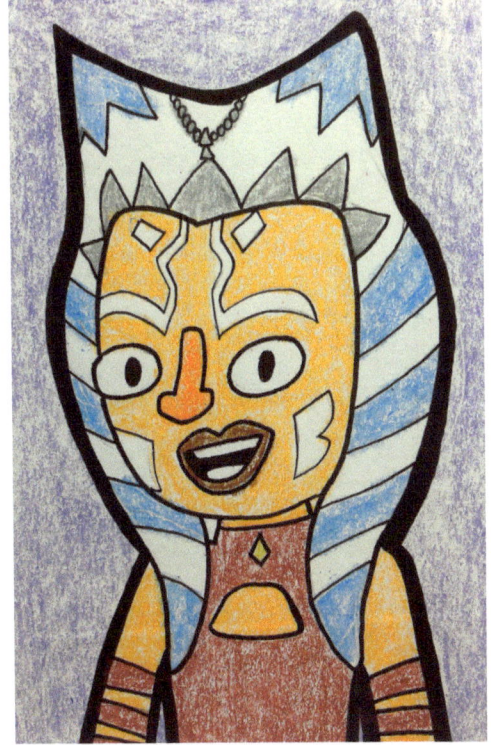

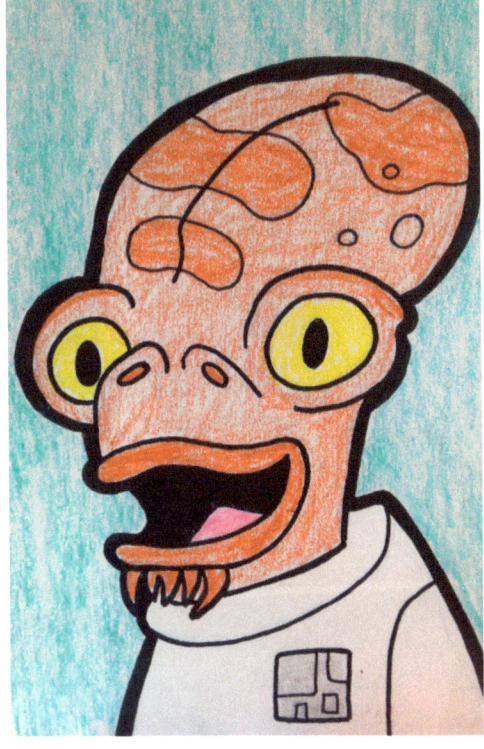

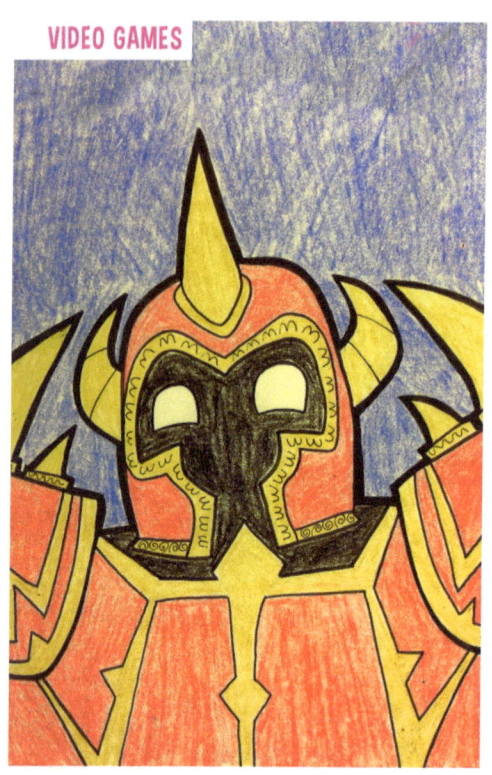

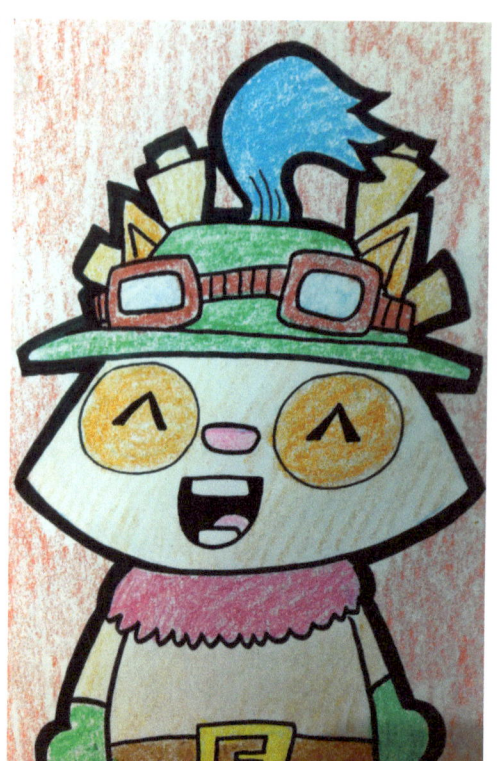

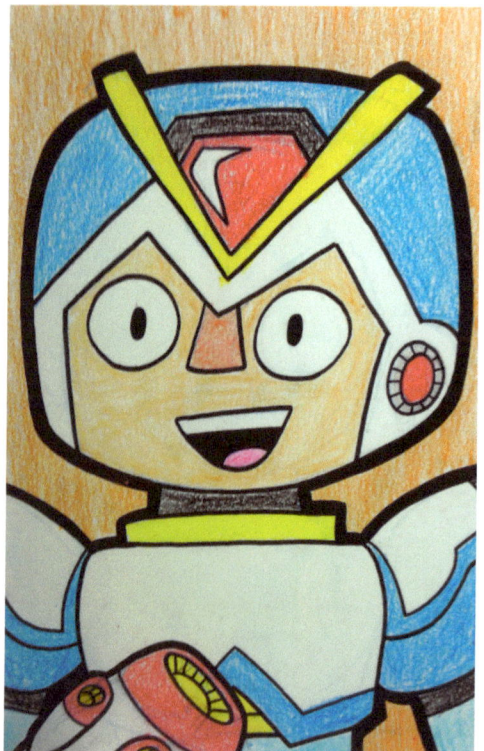

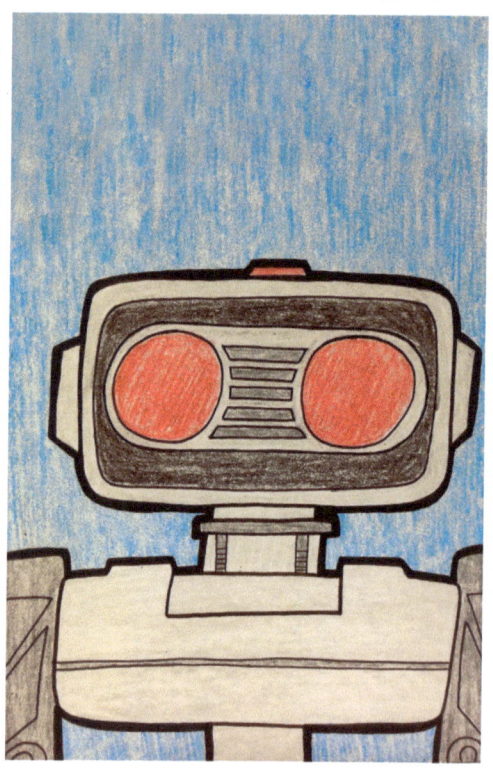

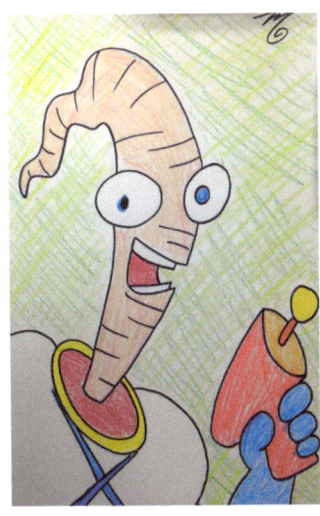
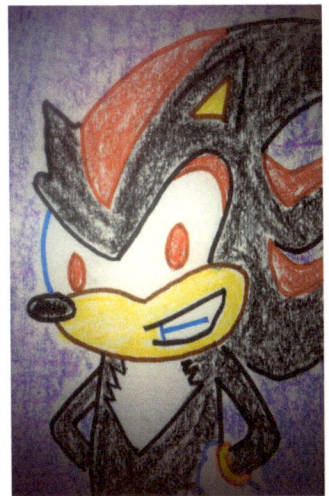
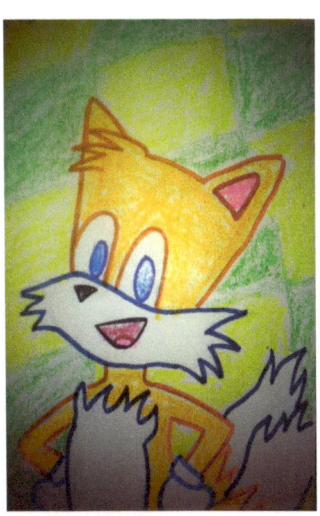
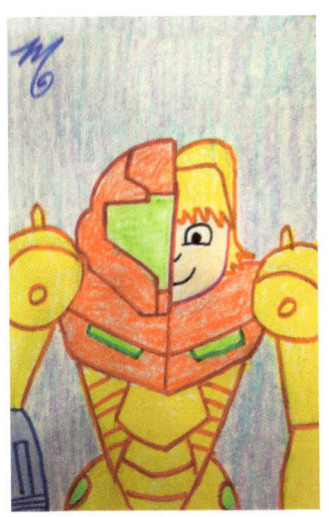
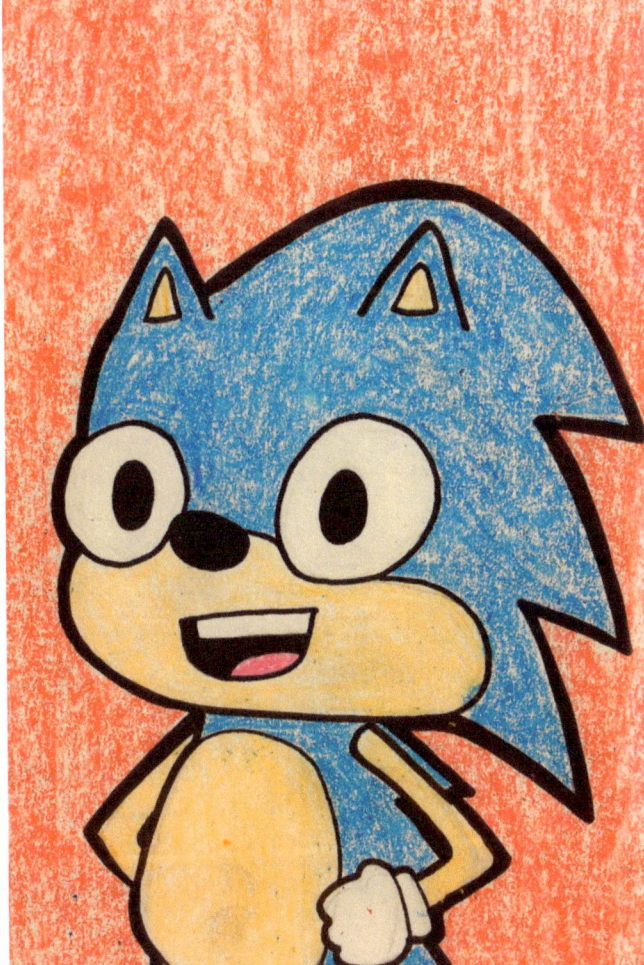

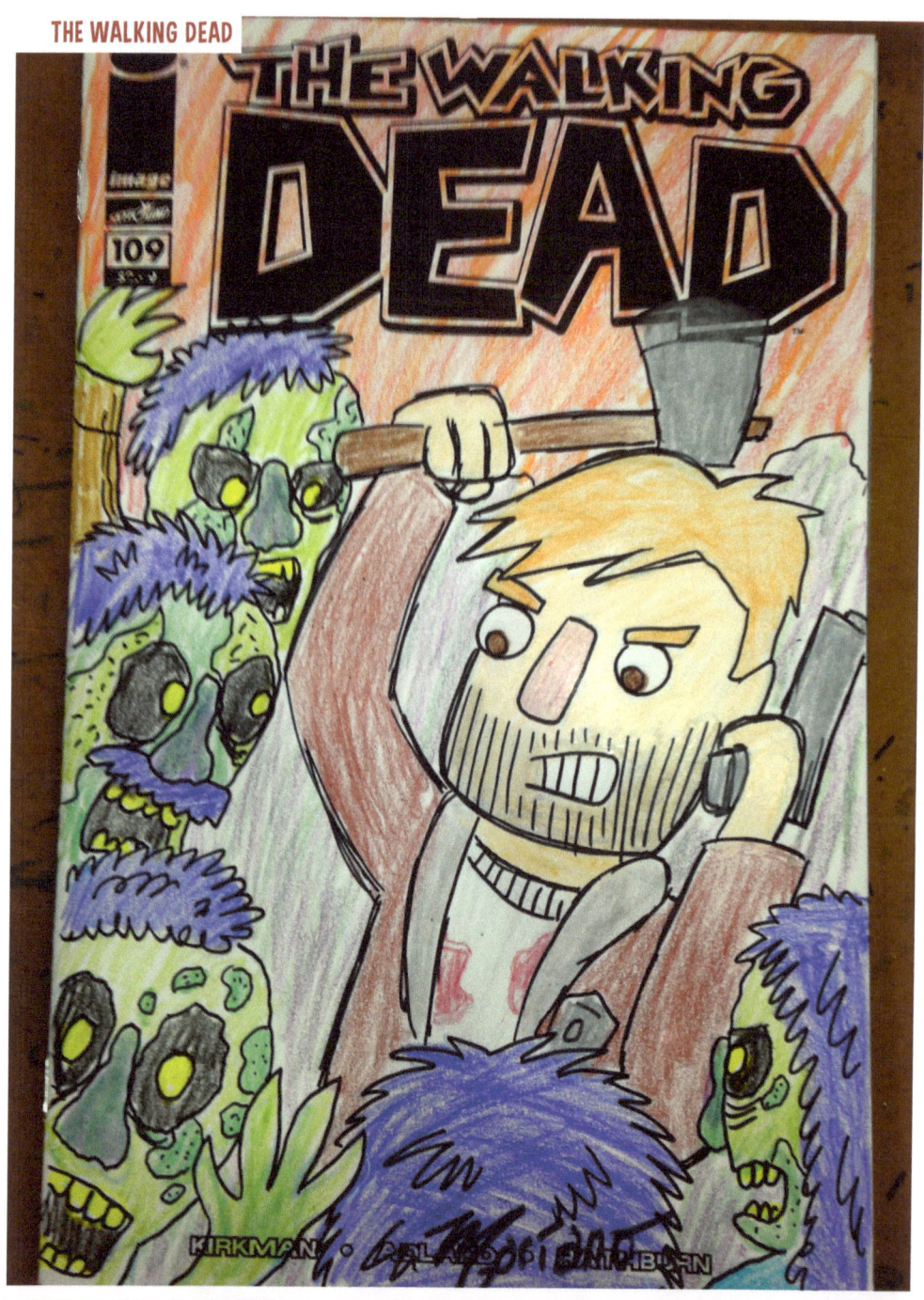

THIS PAGE: The Walking Dead sketch cover

OTHER PAGE: Clementine, Lee Everett, Walkers, Rick Grimes

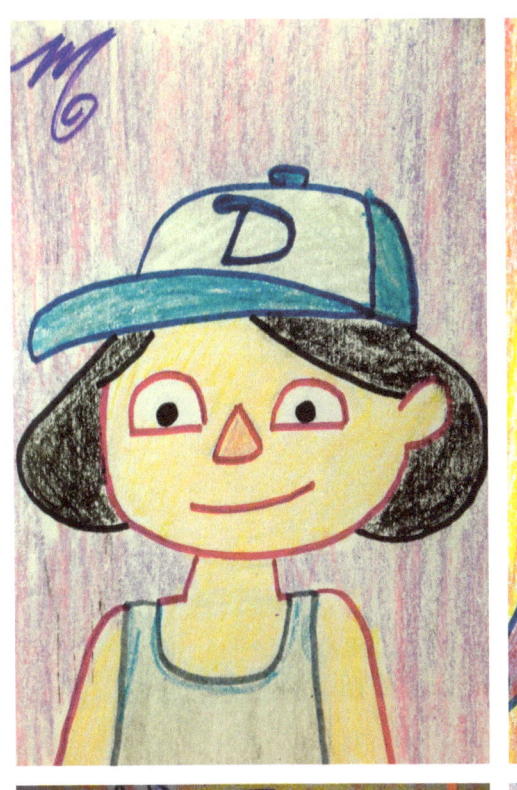
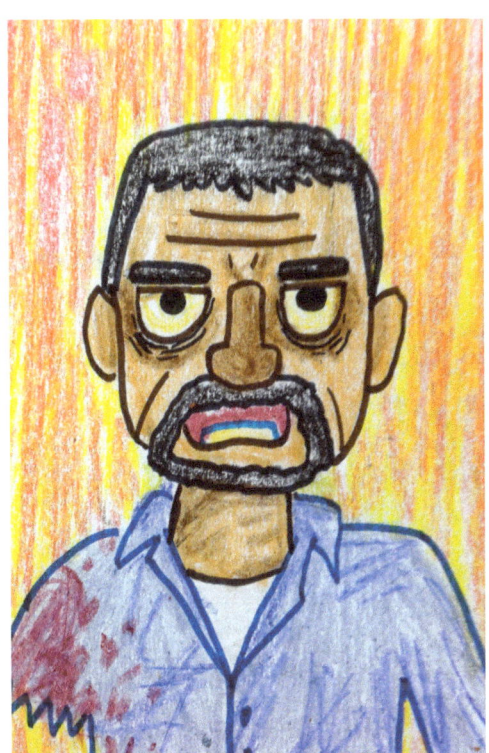
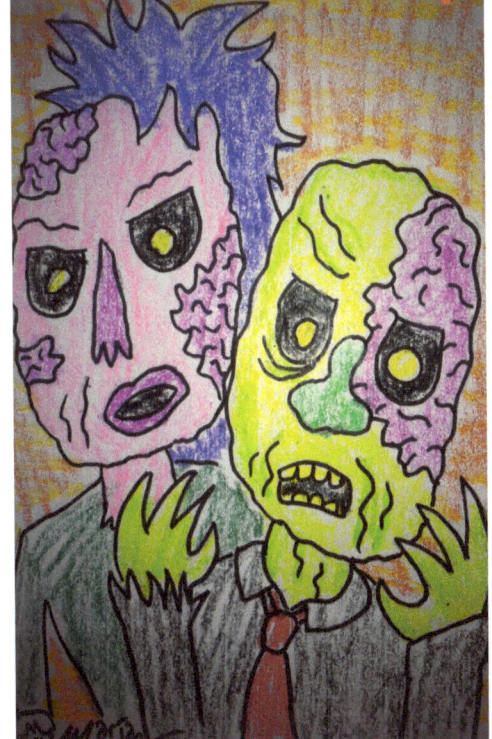
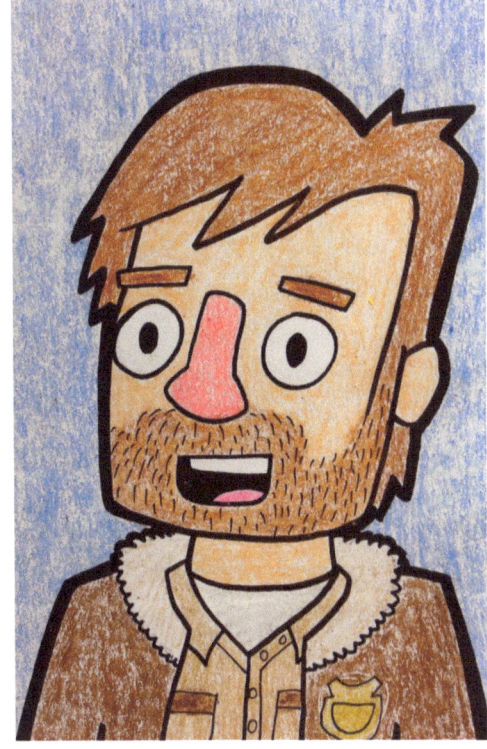

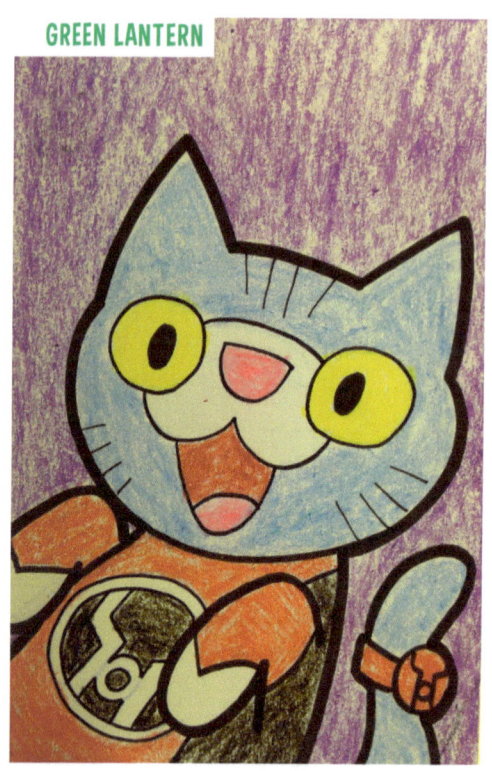
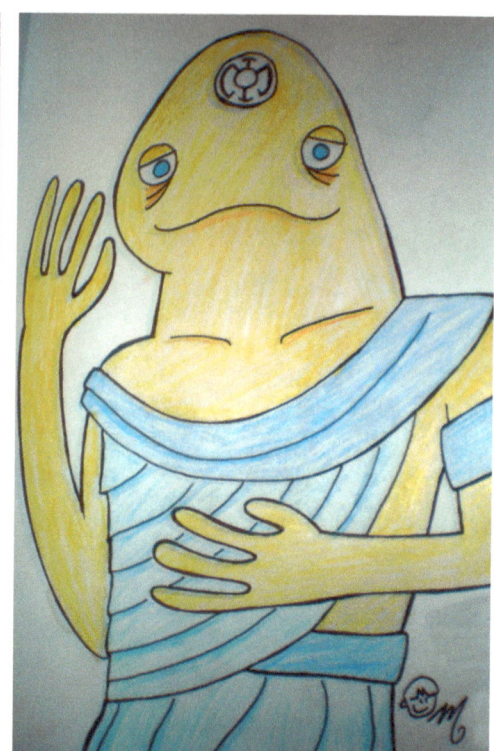
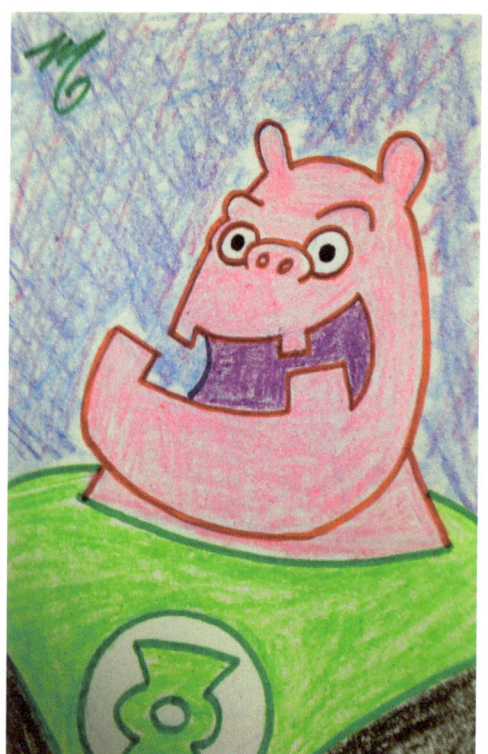
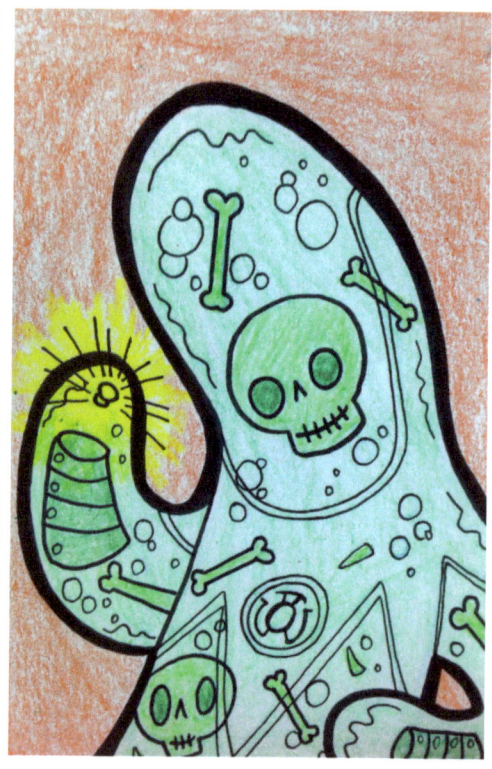

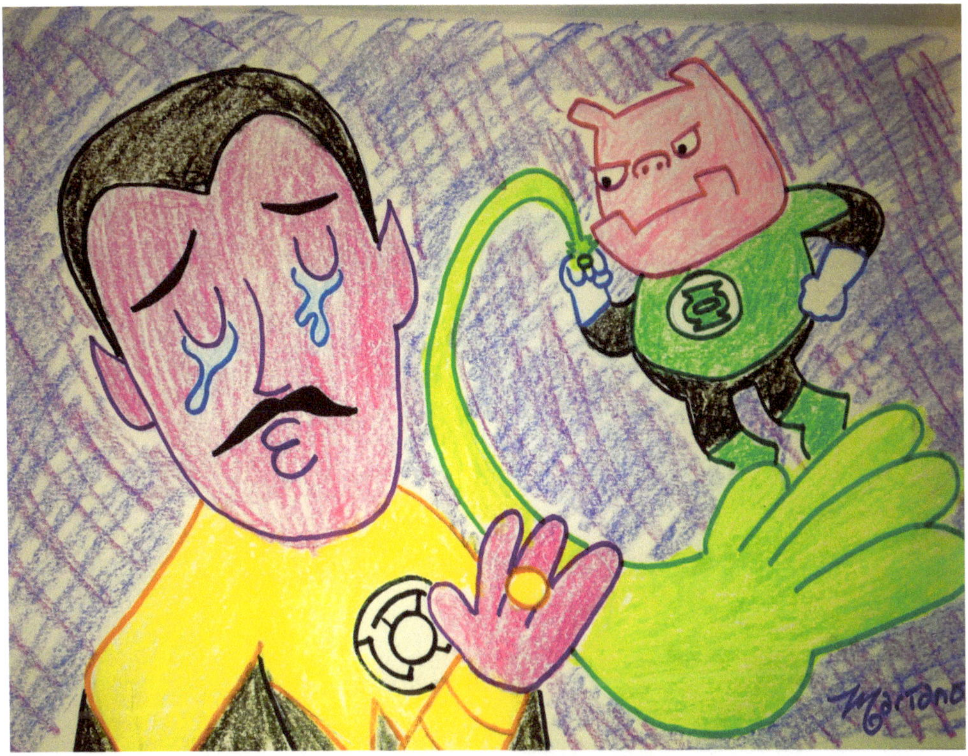

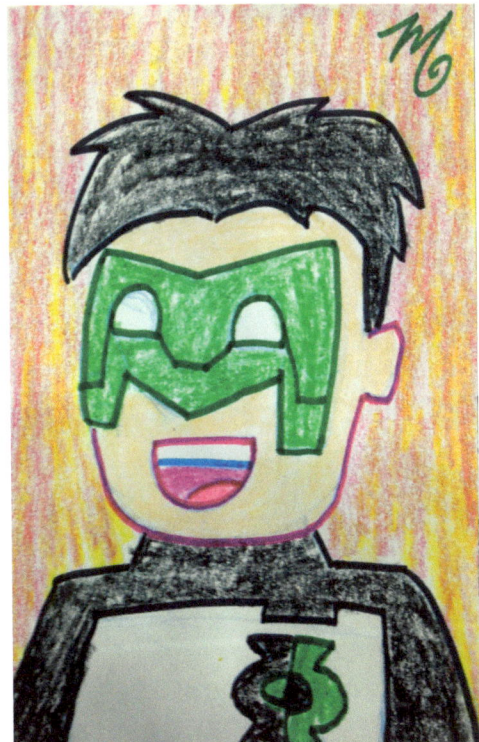
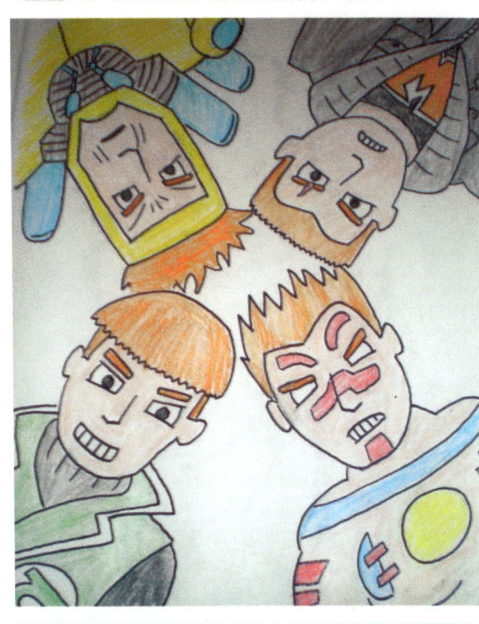

OTHER PAGE: Dex-Starr, Brother Hynn, Kilowog, Slushh
THIS PAGE: Sinestro gets smacked, Kyle Rayner, 4 faces of Guy Gardner

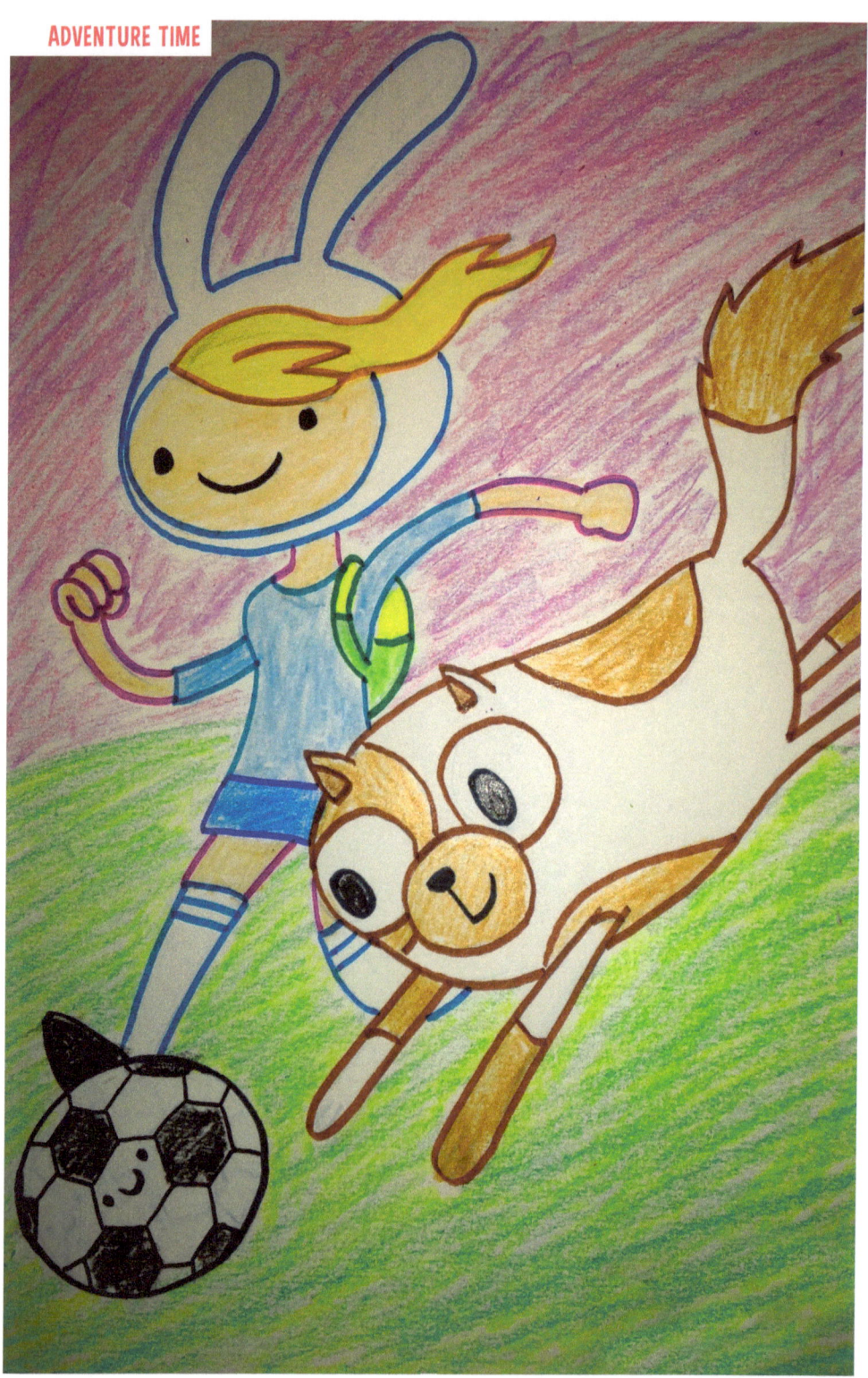

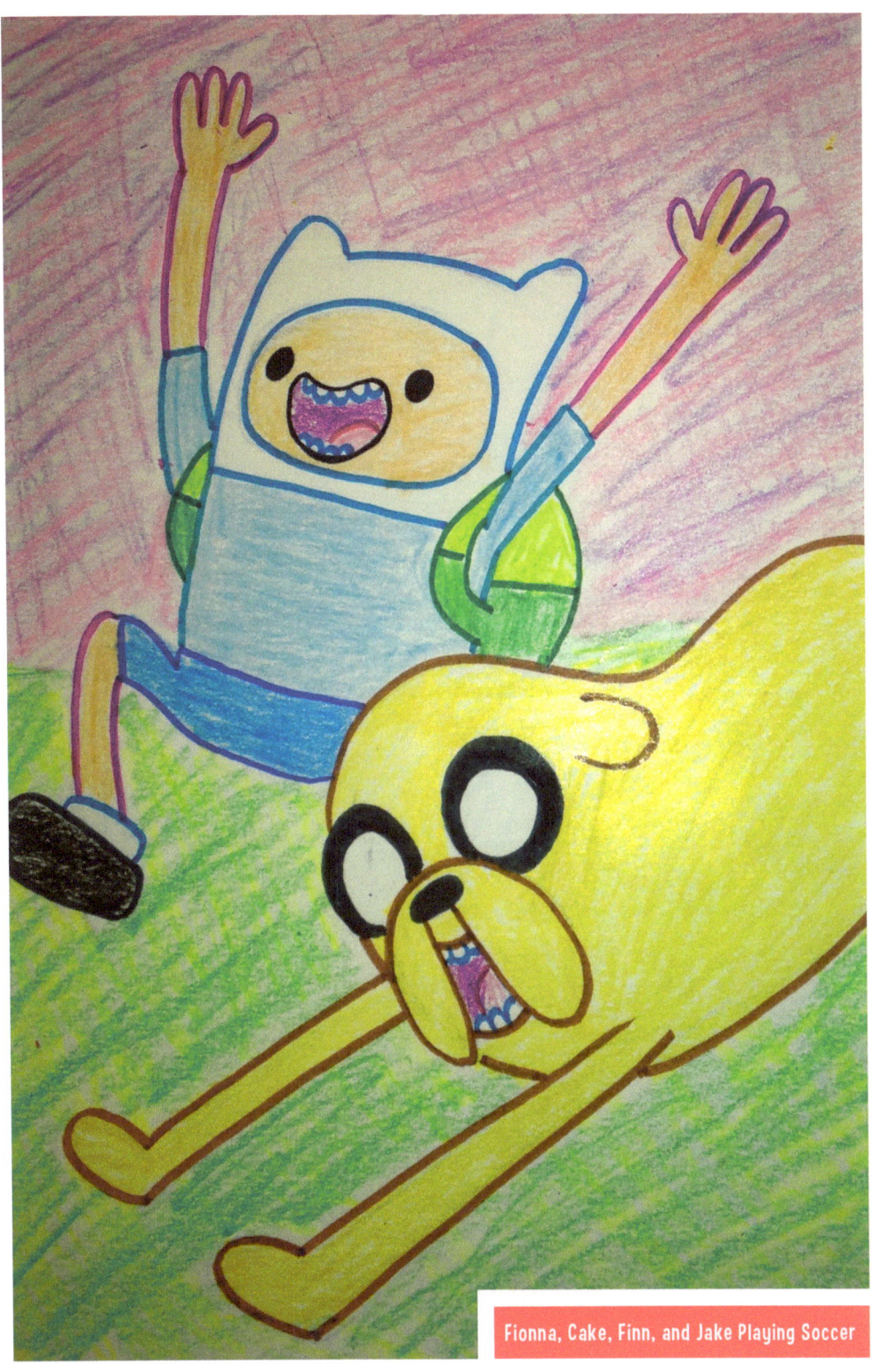

Fionna, Cake, Finn, and Jake Playing Soccer

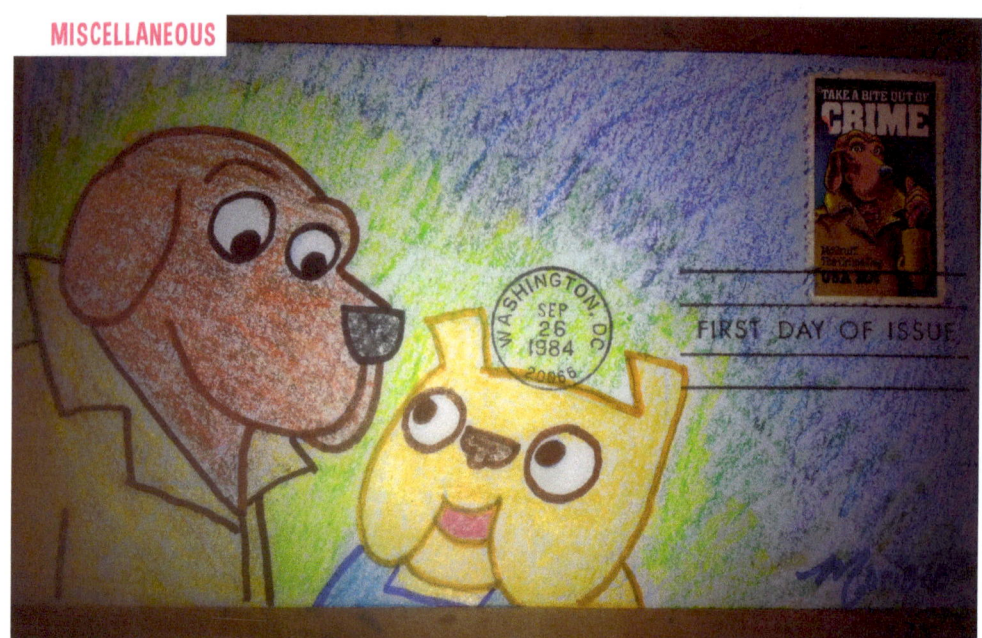

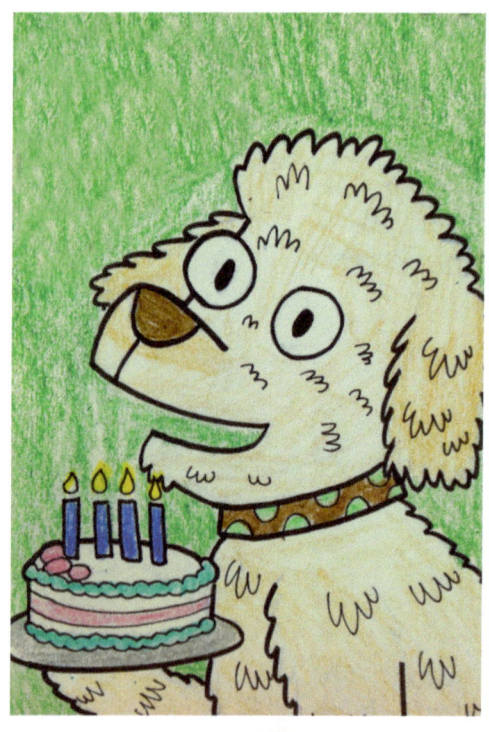

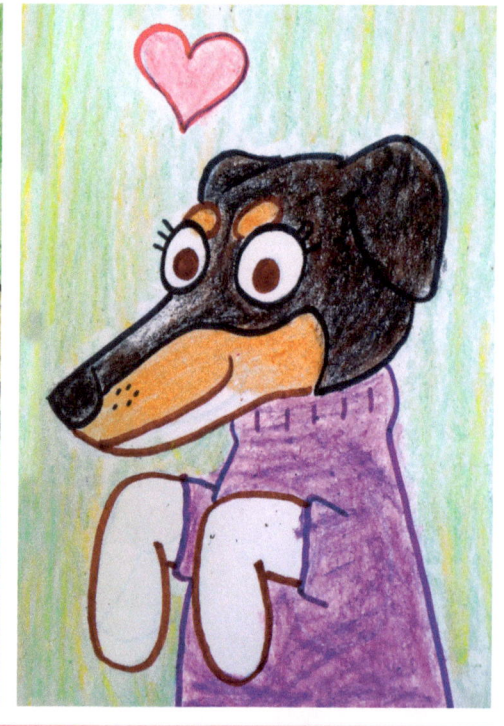

THIS PAGE: McGruff and Meatsauce, Birthday Doggie, Charlotte the Dachshund

OTHER PAGE: Turtleduck, Chrysanthemum, Captain Cold Miser and Heat Wave Miser

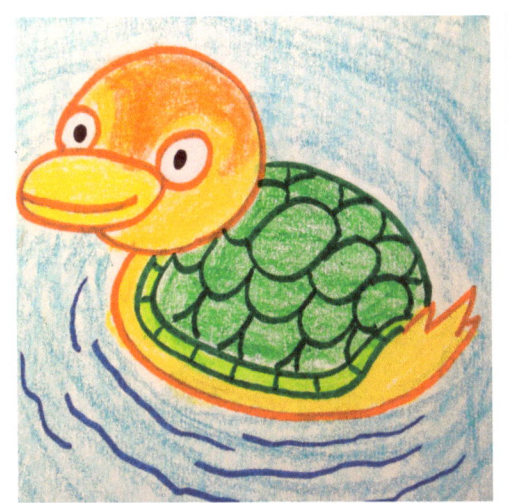
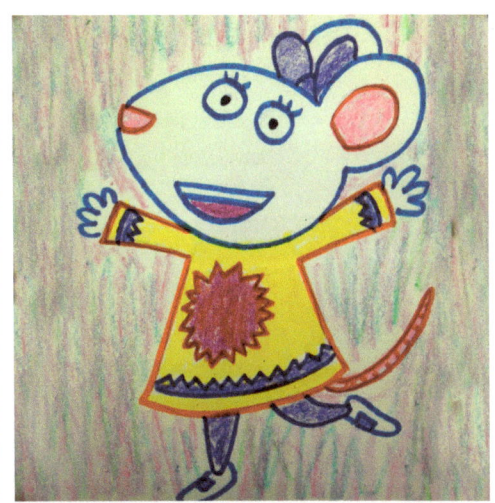

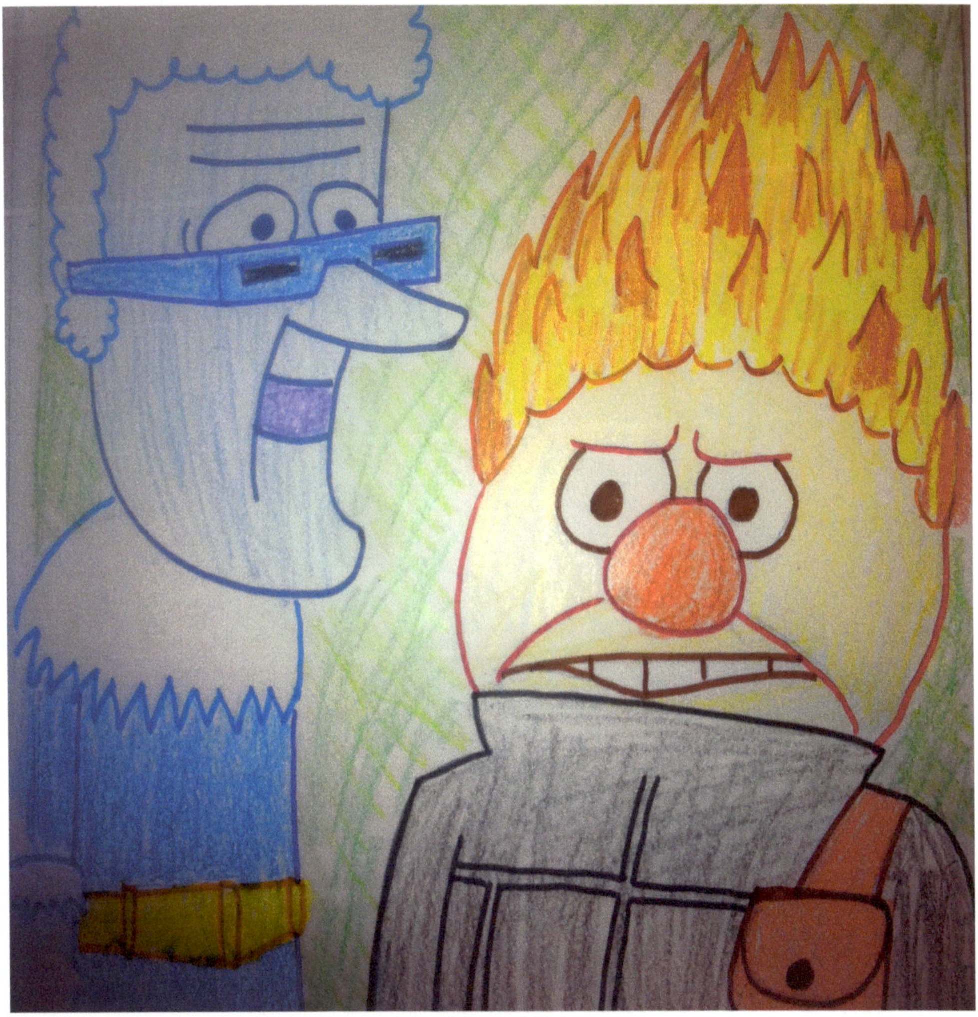

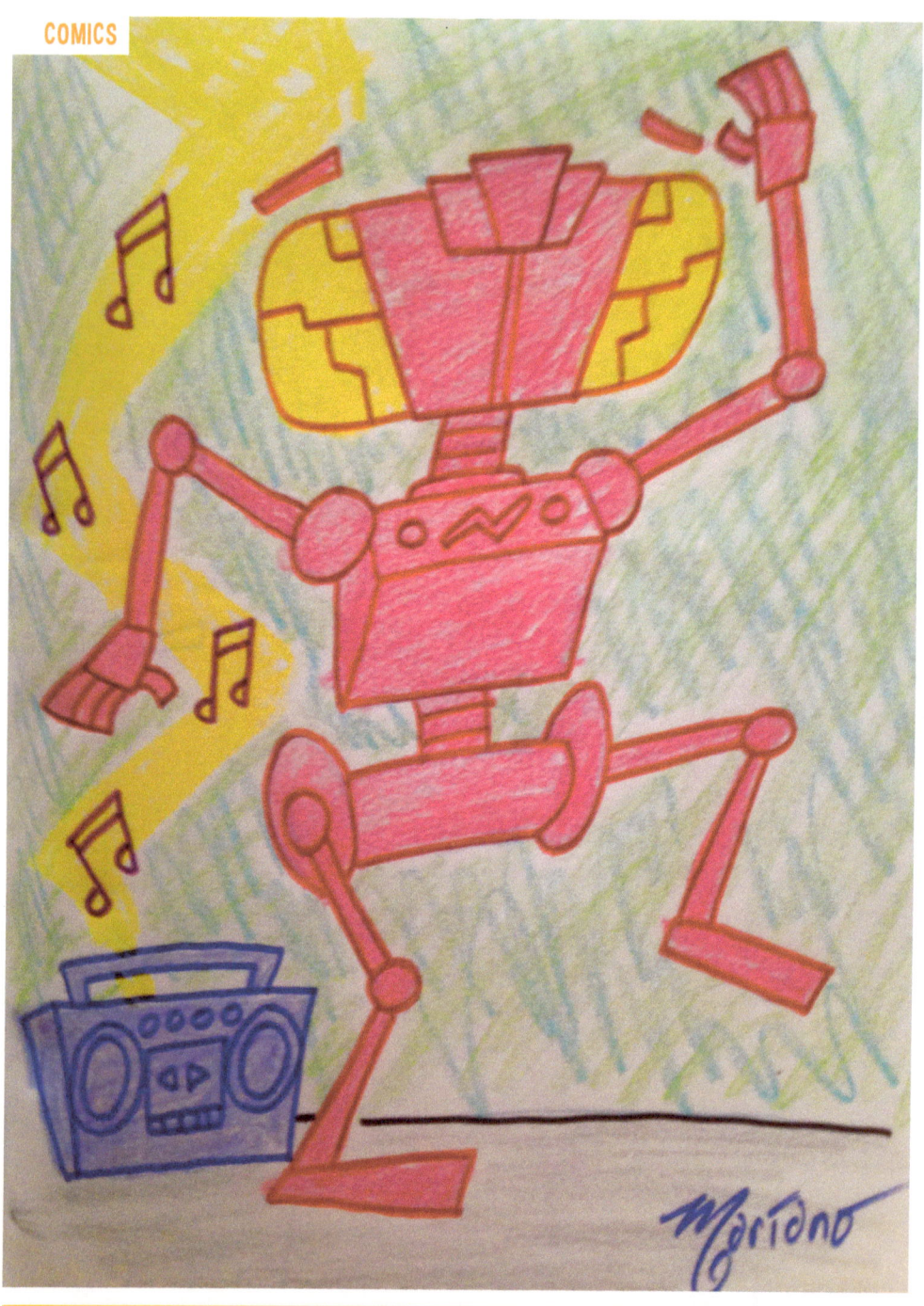

THIS PAGE: L-Ron

OTHER PAGE: Dave Strider, Rogue and Gambit, Spider-Ham, Ozymandias, Jean Grey

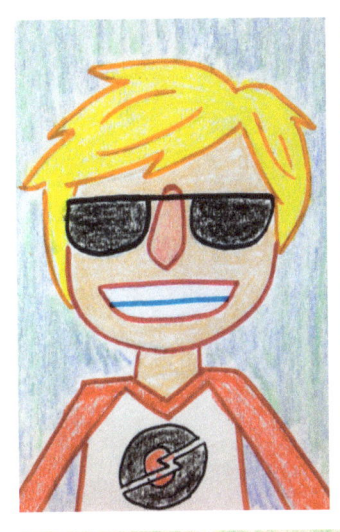

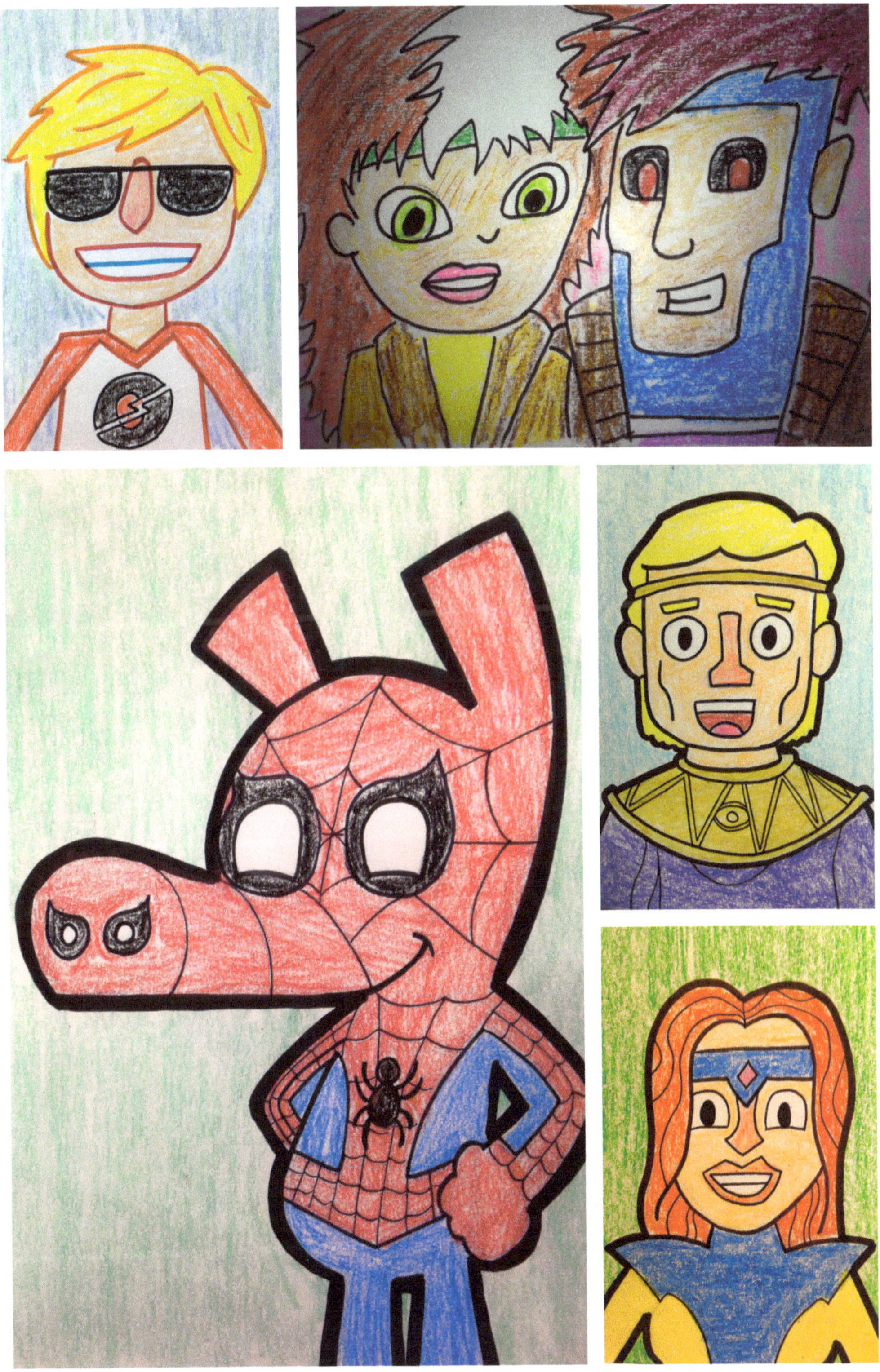

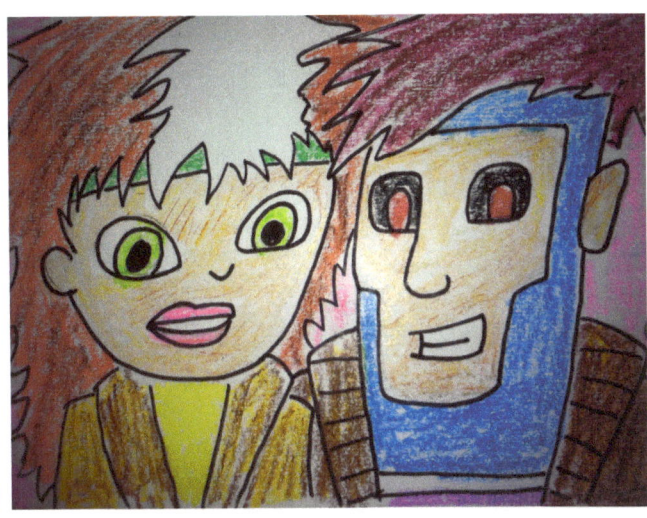

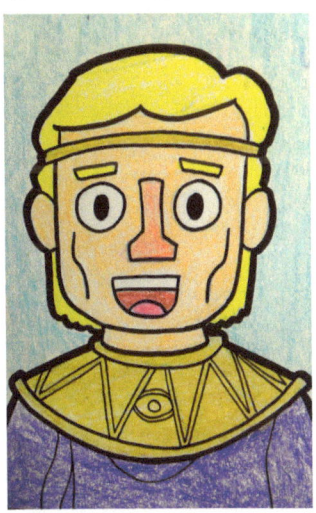

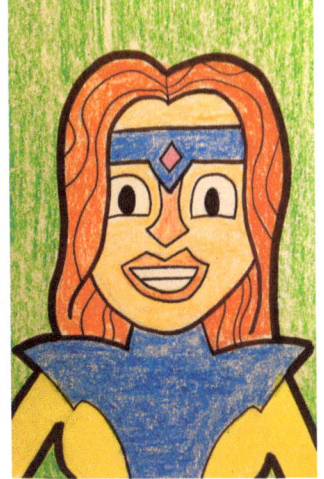

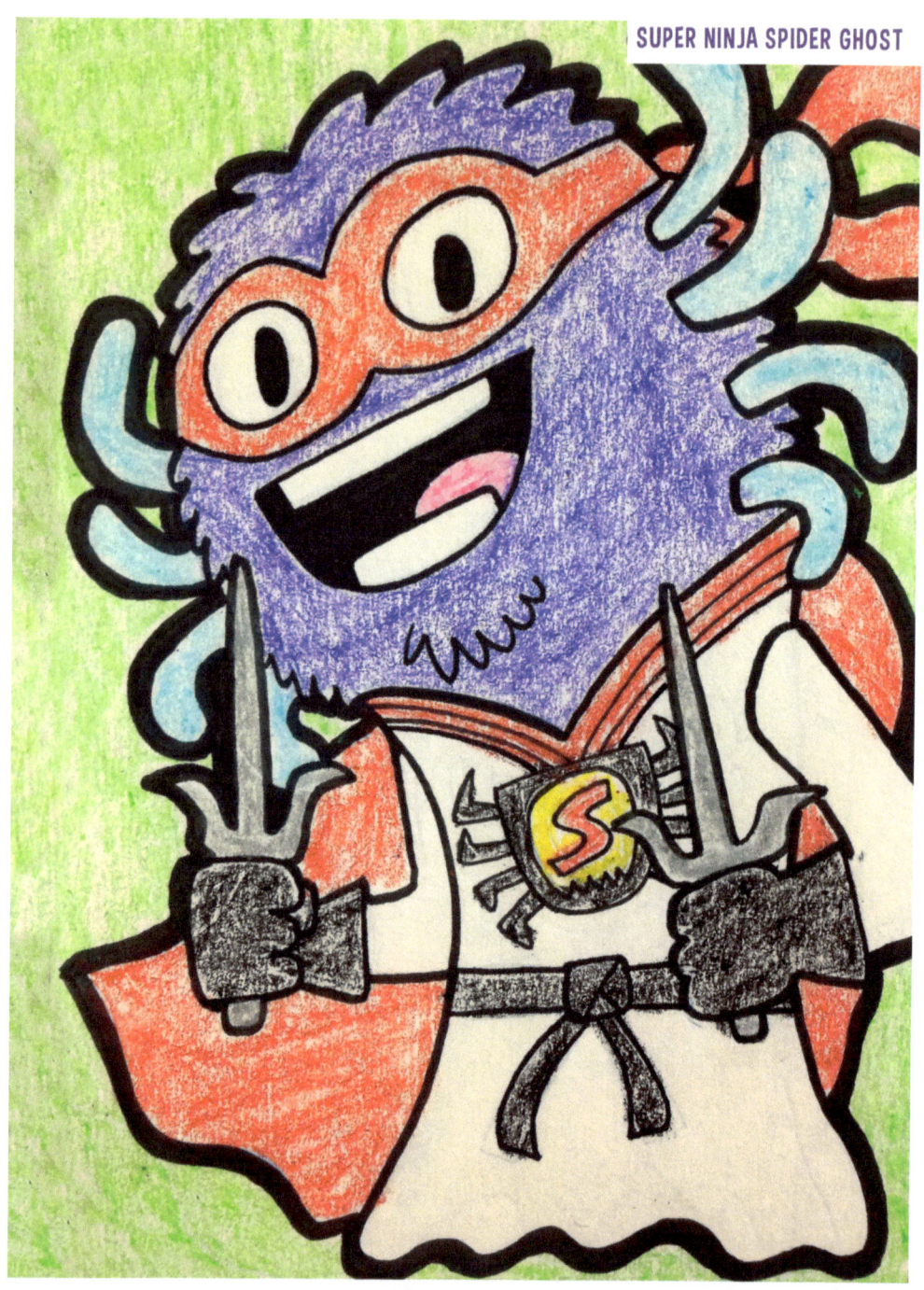

SUPER NINJA SPIDER GHOST